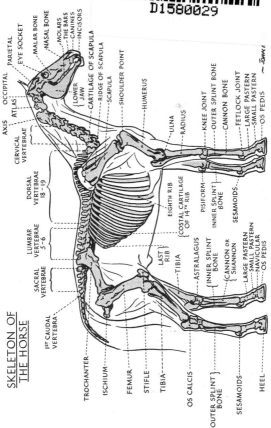

SKELETON OF THE HORSE

PARIETAL
OCCIPITAL
EYE SOCKET
MALAR BONE
NASAL BONE
MOLARS
THE BARS
CANINES
INCISORS
LOWER JAW
AXIS
ATLAS
CARTILAGE OF SCAPULA
RIDGE OF SCAPULA
SCAPULA
SHOULDER POINT
HUMERUS
CERVICAL VERTEBRAE
ULNA
RADIUS
KNEE JOINT
OUTER SPLINT BONE
CANNON BONE
FETLOCK JOINT
LARGE PASTERN
SMALL PASTERN
OS PEDIS
DORSAL VERTEBRAE 18-19
EIGHTH RIB
COSTAL CARTILAGE OF 14TH RIB
PISIFORM
INNER SPLINT BONE
SESAMOIDS
LUMBAR VERTEBRAE 5-6
LAST RIB
TIBIA
ASTRALAGUS
INNER SPLINT BONE
CANNON OR SHANNON
LARGE PASTERN
SMALL PASTERN
NAVICULAR
OS PEDIS
SACRAL VERTEBRAE
1ST CAUDAL VERTEBRA
TROCHANTER
ISCHIUM
FEMUR
STIFLE
TIBIA
OS CALCIS
OUTER SPLINT BONE
SESAMOIDS
HEEL

Observer's Books

The Observer's Book of

HORSES
AND PONIES

R. S. SUMMERHAYS

Revised by
DAPHNE MACHIN GOODALL

DESCRIBING NEARLY 130 BREEDS
AND VARIETIES WITH
98 BLACK AND WHITE ILLUSTRATIONS

FREDERICK WARNE
LONDON

New edition published 1978
by Frederick Warne (Publishers) Ltd, London
Copyright © 1978 Frederick Warne & Co. Ltd.

Reprinted 1979

First published 1949

ACKNOWLEDGEMENTS

Thanks are given to the following copyright owners and photographers for their kind permission to reproduce photographs in this book:

Australian News and Information (p 218); Crown Copyright reserved (p 47); Wayne Dinsmore of the now non-existent Horse and Mule Assn. of America (various photographs); French Government Tourist Office (p 59); the Hayes Estate and Messrs Hurst and Blackett (photographs reproduced from *Points of the Horse*); The Indonesian Embassy in London (p 62); Gilbert H. Jones, president of the Spanish Mustang Registry (p 155); Leslie Lane (p 78); Monty (p 196); Michael Lyster (p 38); D. J. Murphy (Publishers) Ltd (pp 61, 93); John Nestle (pp 33); 'Photonews', Brighton (pp 82,89,176); Scuola di Equitazione, Cagliari, Italy (p 130); Sally Anne Thompson (pp 16,24,25,29,43,51,53,55,64,66,69,75,83, 87,90,94,99,106,107,114,115,117,119,121,123,142,143, 154,160,163,169,184,192,193,202,226,227,230); Werner Menzendorf, Berlin (p 150); The Zoological Society of London (p 237).

ISBN 0 7232 1573 1

Printed in Great Britain by
William Clowes & Sons Limited
Beccles and London
D5820.379

PREFACE

From time to time volumes of considerable size and much detail have been produced on the subject of the Horses and Ponies of the world. It is believed that never before has the subject been compressed within the compass of a book which can be carried in a man's pocket.

The scope of the book being such, the description of each breed needs to be much concentrated. The aim has been to deal in the briefest form with the origin and development of each breed, while at the same time describing its appearance and general character; and, where it exists, the official description issued by the appropriate Breed Society.

Nearly 130 breeds and varieties have been discussed—a particularly impressive number when it is considered how few of these may be looked upon as pure or truly indigenous breeds. Many more breeds or types might have been included; but in each case, after careful consideration and research, it was found that the breed under review was too similar to some other dealt with in these pages, and probably came from the same country.

There is no doubt that the greater number of horses and ponies in the world, though bearing a breed name and, indeed, considered as a distinct breed, are, in fact, part-bred. These, in the main, have been graded-up or refined from probably native stock to meet some agricultural or urban requirement of the country.

My very grateful thanks are offered to Lt.-Col. C. E. G. Hope, Lt. K. Rutczynski, Mrs. Juanita Berlin, Dr. C. W. Grote and Miss Daphne Machin Goodall, M. Jean Froissard, Professor V. Popov, and to Mrs. Stella A. Walker for their assistance. Acknowledgements are also due to *Indian Farming*;

to the late Lady Wentworth, Capt. M. H. Hayes, Maj.-Gen. Sir James Johnstone, Prof. Janikowski, E. Iverton and A. E. Pease, from whose works I have quoted. Thanks are also given to *Pony Owner's Encyclopaedia* for information on the Falabella miniature horse; to Laura Laylin and Louise Firouz, *Pony*, December 1965, and *Light Horse*, April 1966, for material on the Caspian pony; and to *Light Horse* for material on the Bulgarian breeds.

R. S. SUMMERHAYS

This is the preface which the late R. S. Summerhays wrote to his revised edition in 1968. I need only add that during the intervening years new facts about breeds of horses and ponies or their history have come to light and I have tried to include these, as the publishers wished, in the present revised edition. Some of the photographs have been replaced by those of more recent examples of various breeds. It is hoped that the book is in keeping with what the author would have wished.

D.M.G.

THE HORSE-BREEDING
COUNTRIES OF THE WORLD

The Americas and Canada   It is certain that horses, in the main, thrive in Canada, and the fact that its winters are very severe is, on the whole, advantageous for their health.   Nevertheless, this great cold and the comparative shortness of the spring and summer months do not encourage horse-breeding.   It is perhaps mainly for this reason that Canada cannot claim as its own any particular breed of horse.   Therefore, we have to cross the border and go farther south to reach lands where the horse is bred in great numbers and also in a variety of types.   In the pages of this book will be described the many different breeds to be found not only in the United States but also farther south still—in South America.

We will, therefore, proceed south and deal first with the United States of America as a horse-breeding country.   It seems fairly certain that Christopher Columbus was responsible for the re-introduction of the horse into America via the West Indies; but it is also known that the early settlers in the North American continent imported horses.   Later in this book much information is given about specific types of horses and their origin; here we are in the main concerned with the advantages of the United States as a horse-breeding country.   Although the great mountain ranges of the West are not suitable, the many fertile plains elsewhere provide ideal conditions for raising cattle and horses.   It was over such plains as these that, centuries ago, herds of horses ran wild, at times increasing to such an extent that they became a menace.

This great continent indeed enjoys certain extensive areas which are ideal for the growth of the horse at its best; and Americans are particularly proud of the picturesquely named 'Blue Grass Country' of Kentucky, which may roughly be described as lying mid-east. Here, around Lexington, in a land with an adequate but not excessive rainfall and a soil containing sufficient lime and phosphate to stimulate the growth of lush grass, is to be found the ideal nursery for the horse. Here, too, is the home of the flat-racer and trotting horse, as well as many other American breeds.

When we think of South America, our thoughts instinctively turn to the Criollo, the polo pony and the cow pony, all indispensable, immensely tough and indefatigable workers on the estancias. Except in the great mountains on the western side, and where the extremes of temperature are too pronounced, South America has always been admirable horse-raising country. The Spanish expedition of Pizzaro, engaged in the conquest of Peru, had 21 horses, with some later additions, which must have bred at an astonishing rate, for it is known that in a comparatively short time vast herds of these were found in the country just south of the Rio de la Plata. Perhaps these horses had found and intermingled with other wild herds, but this only confirms the fact that the horse thrives in the wild state in that country.

Asia In the description of the breeding grounds of the horse in Asia we include primarily the following regions: Arabia, Syria, Persia, Turkestan, Mongolia, Northern India and China. It is generally considered that this was the original breeding area of the horse as we know it now. It is also found in other parts of Asia—Burma, Assam,

Malaysia, Java, Sumatra—but it is fairly certain that the horse came to those places as an immigrant. As early as 1345 the great traveller Ibn Batuta found no horses in Java. It is generally accepted that the ponies of Central Sumatra, originally named Batak or Deli after the regions where they were bred, are of Arabian and Persian origin. The China pony is probably a cross between the Mongolian and foreign stock, but there were named strains of horses some 1200 years B.C. The ponies of Burma, the Shan States and Manipur, although very ancient breeds, appear to derive from the horses of Mongolia.

Remains of a horse with a skull very similar in some characteristics to that of the Arab have been found in Pliocene deposits of the Siwaliks, the southern foothills of the Himalayas in India. The other prehistoric horse of India is one whose remains were found in the more recent Pleistocene deposits of the valley of the Narbada in Central India, but this may be an ancestral type of the onager or wild ass, rather than of the horse.

The Mongolian influence has spread all over Central Asia, China, Turkestan, the Himalayas, India and the tropical and sub-tropical countries of Asia and Burma, and to Russia and Northern Europe. The Arab blood has flowed to India and South-east Asia, and westwards via North Africa into Europe. The strains probably met in India and in Persia, the horses of which seem descended from those of Turkestan (ex-Mongolian) on the one side and from those of Arabia on the other.

In assessing the geographical and climatic effect of this vast breeding-ground on the horse, it should be noted that the area can roughly be divided into three types of country: the deserts and plains of the west and south-west—Arabia, Persia, Northern India, with great extremes of heat and cold, but mainly with hot, dry climates; the highlands and plateaux of Central Asia, wind-swept and bitterly cold; and the tropical and sub-tropical regions of South-east Asia—Burma, Malaysia, Java, Sumatra, with their extreme humidity and little variation of temperature. The first two areas had—and still have—one common feature which made them suitable for horses, wide, open spaces where they could roam at large and use their speed to escape from enemies.

The country is generally arid, with wide areas of desert and barren country, stony of soil and containing a certain amount of limestone, on which, as we know, the horse has always flourished. Grazing and fodder is generally scarce except in oases and cultivated districts; but in all these regions, Arabia especially, a good crop of grass and herbage springs up after rain.

It may be remarked here that all attempts to establish a firm breed of Indian country-bred without the continual re-introduction of outside blood has failed. After the second generation the progeny begin to revert in size and appearance to the original type. Nor, so far as we know, has the horse ever been seriously used for draught in India, its place invariably being taken by oxen.

Western and Central Asia were by climate and geography well suited, up to a point, to be a breeding-ground for the horse. The limitations imposed by temperature and pasturage produced the horse best adapted for the conditions—small and wiry, with feet like iron and an ability to survive on a sparse diet.

It is appropriate here to mention the Libyan horse, the Barb, because the terrain of North Africa, from which it comes, is very similar to that just described and was certainly one of the routes by which the Arab reached Europe. Indigenous horses are known to have existed in the river valleys of North-west Africa—apparently of a strain similar to that of horses of the valleys of Southern Spain. At one time Spain was joined to North Africa.

The south-western and tropical regions of Asia did not produce an indigenous horse, and the one introduced remained small in size and generally of thicker and more solid build than that of the open desert spaces.

It is impossible to go into much detail in a short survey such as this, but enough has been said, perhaps, to give a general idea of the vast area and of the horses it has produced, and where the horse was first tamed. It may be interesting to note that the earliest known treatise on the horse is believed to come from Mesopotamia, the Hittite *Hippologica Hethitica*, which was inscribed on clay tablets about 1360 B.C. The book deals with the care of horses used for war and racing chariots.

Australasia The horse is bred now in all parts of Australasia, but attention will necessarily be concentrated on Australia, as the principal breeding-ground. It is interesting to note that all this area, so admirably suited for horses, had never known one until it was introduced by man in the late 18th century.

The general physical formation of Australia is a coastal plain rising fairly easily to barrier ranges of mountains, higher in the east than in the west, with an enormous central plain, partly waterless desert and partly scrub, and a moderately high habitable plateau in the hinterland of Western Australia. The coastal plains and highlands of the east, on either side of the mountain barriers, are generally well watered and temperate in climate, and have good and varied pasture, and plenty of limestone in the soil. It is here that the 'Waler', the horse of Australia, has reached its highest pitch of breeding and performance, especially in New South Wales, and to a lesser extent in Queensland and Victoria. Here, too, almost every variety of good sized English light and heavy horse is produced, and here, of course, racing flourishes. Australia is also the home *par excellence* of the high jumper.

In Western Australia the climate is very dry, subject to great extremes of temperature, and tends to resemble to some extent that of Arabia and North India. There is plenty of good grazing and scrub land and good limestone content in the soil. The horses of Western Australia are descendants of the Java and East Indian pony, having been imported from Timor and elsewhere, and remain peculiar to this part of Australia. The effect of temperature on size is here clearly shown, these animals remaining as ponies while those of the more temperate east grow to full size.

New Zealand also has favourable climatic and geographical conditions for the breeding of horses: wide ranges, good rolling grasslands with excellent pasturage and limestone content. Horses were introduced there at about the same time as they were to Australia, a fair amount of the stock coming from Australia itself. Although recently horse-breeding has been carried out with increasing enthusiasm, it has never been the serious business that it became in Australia.

The British Isles and Ireland   Better suited for it than many other parts of the world, Britain and Ireland have always been great regions for horse-breeding.   No doubt this happy position is largely due to the climate—in which no extremes of heat are met with and where there is abundant moisture to encourage the growth of rich grasslands. The soil, even without much artificial attention, tends to grow just the nutricious and abundant grass which normally produces in horses the bulk and density of bone that is of primary importance to their work and well-being.

The British Isles are unique in having so many truly indigenous breeds; there are, indeed, no fewer than nine, each one indigenous to a particular district and in appearance dissimilar from the others.   They have, however, shared characteristics, those of small size, great hardiness, surefootedness, intelligence and the ability to feed and thrive on rough upland country.   These breeds are the Shetland and Highland of Scotland, the Fell and Dales of Northern England, the Welsh Mountain Pony from Wales, the Exmoor and Dartmoor from the extreme South-west, and the New Forest from Southern England. Ireland can claim only one indigenous breed, the good Connemara.

In Scotland the climate is, generally speaking, too severe for the profitable breeding of horses; in the main, only breeds such as the Shetland and Highland can stand up to it.   We must not, however, forget the Clydesdale, that massive but active agricultural and commercial horse, which emanated from the South of Scotland.

Travelling southward, we come to the famous

horse-breeding grounds of Yorkshire, from which Thoroughbreds, Hunters, the Yorkshire Coach Horse and the Cleveland Bay, not to mention the Hackney, have come in great numbers. Still farther south, the 'shires' provide ideal nurseries for any type of horse. This would include, therefore, the heavy breeds, for these parts are the home of England's great Shire horses.

The Eastern Counties are the home of the clean-legged cart-horses, the Suffolk, or Punch, and the Percheron, a comparatively new importation. Most important of all, the Eastern Counties have within their borders Newmarket, the headquarters of racing. The very home of the world-famous English Thoroughbred, Newmarket has sent out from its classic paddocks the finest racehorses the world has ever seen.

Throughout Southern England, except perhaps in the extreme South-west, are to be found many famous Thoroughbred studs and training establishments, including in particular those tucked away in the rolling Wiltshire Downs, and in the glorious South Downs which strike across the southern part of Sussex.

In this general survey of the horse-breeding countries, it can be said with confidence that Ireland's reputation is second to none for producing the best-boned, the most healthy and the most generally desirable stock from which to breed. The most favoured part of Ireland is the South-east, where great numbers of Thoroughbreds have been foaled and where the best of that typical Irish horse, the part-bred hunter type, has been bred.

Continental Europe From prehistoric times different types of horses inhabited the plains, forests and mountains of Europe. Five of these types are depicted on the walls of the cave at Lascaux in France.

Predominantly there was a cob type, known to later hippologists as the diluvial horse, although now it is called by the scientific name of *Equus robustus*; the present Asiatic wild horse or Przevalsky horse, *Equus przevalskii przevalskii* Poliakoff; and the forest and steppe Tarpans, *Equus przevalskii gmelini* Antonius, *forma sylvaticus*, if the forest type is meant. These were, generally speaking, the ancestors of most of the pony breeds of Europe, whilst the steppe Tarpan was to be the ancestor of the fine-limbed Eastern horses. Naturally these early primitive types crossed and so, in turn, strains evolved.

Typical representatives of the so-called 'hot-bloods' are the Barb, Arab, and the English Thoroughbred. The Arab and the Thoroughbred are today bred with the greatest care all over Europe—and, indeed, the world—not only for racing purposes but as essential material for the improvement of European local breeds.

In Hungary new half-breeds, such as Nonius and Gidrans, were created with the help of the English Thoroughbred, while Shagya was based on Arabian blood.

In France current policy classifies breeds as the French-bred English Thoroughbred, the Anglo-Arab with a minimum of 25 per cent Arab blood, and the French Saddle Horse, including all half-bred horses raised in France, e.g., the Anglo-Norman, Charollais, Limousin, and Vendéen-Charentais.

Poland has mostly half-bred horses with some Eastern ancestry, and both European Russia and

Poland have now a number of selective breeds of 'warm-blood' horses. In the 8th century when the Moors invaded Spain on Berber and Arab horses, this Eastern blood found its way into the early strains of Spanish and French horses. Thus the Spanish Ginete was created and, through the Spanish horse, the Neapolitan, now extinct, which was bred near Naples, and the Kladruber of Hungary, formerly bred to draw the State coaches and now used in agriculture.

Equus robustus was found throughout Europe and had evolved into a strong short-legged cobby horse. It became the horse of chivalry when knights required war horses and, although certainly not a large animal, it was up to considerable weight and possessed an active gait. About a century ago, when countries first became industrialized, very large strong horses were required for draught and thus the heavy breeds of horses for agriculture were also created. The Percheron lives not only in Perche or in Belgium—which breeds perhaps the best Percheron—but in many other parts of Europe and the world. In the same way the Swedish Ardennes is the most popular breed in Sweden, where, together with the North-Swedish horse, it is found to be very useful in the forestry industry.

The two remaining groups of horses, the Mongolian steppe horse and the North European plateau horse, or Tarpan, are the ones least influenced by man. They are still to be found in their original habitats. While 'cold-blood', 'hot-blood', and 'warm-blood' horses are usually bred in more or less artificial conditions and under the strict supervision of man, steppe horses are bred in *kossiak*, which embraces about 20 mares and a stallion.   A number of *kossiaks* make a *tabun*. In Russia this *tabun* horse-breeding has been adopted on a large scale.

According to local conditions, in which soil and climate play an enormously important part, different breeds were established by crossing with other types and strains of horses or ponies. All of them, however, retained many characteristics of the ancient Tarpan, such as great hardiness, satisfaction with the poorest food, great strength for their size, prepotency and longevity.   They are mostly dun-coloured, with a black dorsal stripe and black mane and tail.

The North European horse has many representatives in Europe, such as the Scottish Highland pony, Shetland, Finnish and Swedish ponies, Russian Viatka pony, Smudish, and mountain pony (huçul).

This is one of the most ancient breeds evolved by the 'Teké' and Turkoman tribe in the oases of southern Turkmenia. Owing to the arid desert conditions, these Akhal-Teké horses, from time immemorial, have been tethered and hand-fed with a mixture of lucerne and barley. They are specialized saddle-horses bred to exist under conditions of great heat and privation. Their conformation is elegant in the extreme, with beautiful heads, a noble expressive eye, long fine necks, and the best of legs and feet. They might be termed the greyhound among horses. Bays and greys are known, but the most desired is a pale honey-gold, with black points.

Many breeds of animals and birds produce from time to time pure white specimens, and the white or Albino horse, which is of course a colour type, not a breed, has since 1937 been fostered and developed in the United States by the American Albino Horse Club. The foundation sire is said to have been 'Old King', foaled in 1906, with breeding unknown, though he is believed to have been of Arabian-Morgan stock. Although with very careful selection, particularly in regard to colour, any type of Albino horse can be developed, whether for riding or for draught, since 'Old King' is regarded as the foundation sire, and as a great many Albino horses used for circuses and parades are descended from him, a short description is desirable.

This horse was 15·2 hands high and strongly built. No dark spots appeared on his skin, which was of the necessary pink colour, and his hair was snow-white and silky, both mane and tail being very full. Possessed of sound endurance and of a vigorous character, he had nevertheless a quiet disposition; his action was commanding and his intelligence considerable. He is further described as having had a short, heavily muscled back with a well-rounded, close-ribbed body, legs of flat bone and white hair around the hoofs.

Albino horses are bred for those to whom a white horse appeals, and naturally many are used for ceremonial purposes and in the circus ring. Such being the case, a large number of these horses have been taught the traditional acts of the performing horse, and the claim that the Albino is a horse of exceptional intelligence may well be based on this. That it is a beautiful horse is true enough, but it must be remembered that as a ceremonial or circus horse it is shown at its best and is exhibited in ideal surroundings and handled expertly—advantages which many other horses do not enjoy.

It is claimed of this line of Albino horses that the stock is very prepotent, particularly in regard to colour, and that even when crossed with coloured mares they produce many beautiful snow-white foals. If, as is supposed, 'Old King' was of Arabian-Morgan stock, this prepotency can well be understood, for this is a marked characteristic of both those breeds.

Breed Society: The American Albino Horse Club.

An interesting example of breeding for a particular purpose is the American Quarter Horse. It began in Virginia in very early days, where, owing to the lack of cleared sites for proper race-courses, the first horse-racing in America was carried on along short improvised tracks called 'race paths', which were in fact cut out of the virgin wilderness. These tracks were usually about a quarter of a mile long (0·4 km), and so the horse which was bred to race on these tracks was called the 'Quarter Horse'.

For this type of racing a very quick starter and fast sprinter was required, and in due course a specific type was produced, originally from a cross of Thoroughbred stallions and native mares.

These latter were no doubt mostly of Spanish origin from stock brought in from Florida through the Carolinas, but some were of Thoroughbred blood.

From a genealogical point of view the Quarter breed starts from an English Thoroughbred, 'Janus', which flourished in Virginia and North Carolina between 1756 and 1780. His distance in England was actually 6·4 km (4 miles), but curiously enough his progeny in America were generally noted for their speed over short distances, and had few equals in quarter-racing. 'Janus' stood 14·2 hands, and his outstanding physical characteristic was his heavy and powerful hindquarters, with great, prominent muscles. The breed that he propagated still exists and is officially known as the American Quarter Horse.

The special points of these horses are closeness to the ground, tremendous power, heavy frames extremely well muscled up, especially in the hindquarters, loin and back. The withers, it should be noted, are low. The height of stallions is usually about 15 hands, and weight nearly 544 kg (1,200 lb). They have great speed from 180 to 400 metres (200 to 400 yards), which is their limit. They are much favoured by cattle men for the work of rounding up cattle, as their fast starting and sprinting enable them to head any beast quickly, and are combined with nimbleness and weight and strength, giving them power to hold a heavy steer when it is roped. In addition, they possess a calmness of temperament which is not affected by sudden starts and changes of speed, and they have the ability to do well on any kind of food.

Breed Society: American Quarter Horse Association.

This breed is a peculiarly Transatlantic product, and one in which Americans take great pride. It emanates from the early pioneering days of the first settlement of the country c. 350 years ago, when there were only two means of movement across the vast distances of the new continent—water and horseback. There was no indigenous horse in America, so the early settlers, like the Spaniards, brought their own or imported them soon after. English amblers and pacers went out before the days of the Thoroughbred, together with horses from Spain, France, Africa and the East. All these went to make up the American Saddle Horse.

The pioneers had to have a light, strong, hardy,

speedy animal, comfortable to ride over long distances, adaptable to harness, good-tempered and intelligent. Accordingly they bred, with careful selection, from the best stock available, including in due course the English Thoroughbred, which gave the breed its fire and brilliance; while it inherited the gentleness and easy gaits of the older English amblers. Various other American stocks have been introduced in the course of time, Morgan, Standard Bred (which are both dealt with in this book) and so on; but the officially designated founder of the present type is the Thoroughbred 'Denmark' (foaled 1839). It is well to note, however, that the parent of the breed, the Kentucky Saddle Horse, was an established product before that time. The blood of 'Messenger', the ancestor of the American trotter, also runs in this breed.

The points of the breed are as follows. Height 15 to 16 hands, preferably not more. In conformation it should be light and elegant, with a good head, long, fine neck, well-sloped shoulders, round barrel, flat croup and good clean legs. The general appearance must be one of breeding and brilliance, with high, proud carriage of head and tail and a stance that covers plenty of ground. In character it must be docile and intelligent.

The speciality of the breed is the gaits which it exhibits in the show-ring, for which it is now almost exclusively bred. These gaits are the usual walk, trot and canter, and also the artificial paces, the running walk, stepping pace or slow rack and the fast rack. Animals are specially trained in each gait, and are known as three- or five-gaited horses according to training. The trot must be highly collected, with the head well flexed, neck and tail arched. The action must be high and smooth and speedy. The rack is a single-footed pace, each foot coming down singly and with great speed, a steady 1–2–3–4 with no pauses, each beat being equal. The stepping pace is really a very old pace often seen in local animals in India and the East and in a good trotting camel, the feet on each side following each other instead of stepping diagonally as in the ordinary trot. These gaits performed with the grace and precision for which the breed is famed are a spectacle not easily forgotten.

The characteristic carriage of the tail is obtained by nicking the muscles of the dock and then setting it in position with a crupper.

With its dynamic action, its three or five gaits, not to mention the peculiar and unnatural set of its tail, this horse is very arresting. And those that reach the highest standard in America present a horse in action comparable only with hackney horses and ponies. The breed can be found only in a few places outside America, nor is it likely ever to receive any measure of popularity were it brought to England, especially now that the law in this country prohibits the nicking and docking of horses' tails.

The American Saddle Horse, as the name implies, is of course used primarily for saddle work, but as the action of this horse is high and exaggerated in the extreme it is unlikely to find general favour anywhere else in the world where the smooth, low, long and level action is considered as the ideal.

Breed Society: American Saddle Horse Breeders Association.

The Iberian (Spanish) horses were light, clever and sure-footed. Crossed with the Barb, they became known as the Andalusian, taking the name of the province in the south of Spain where they were bred. There were two types, the light Ginete and the heavier Villanos, but the latter were chiefly bred in Castile. The Andalusian horse has been further crossed with French and English blood, but it has retained the Barb head.

It is a strong bodied horse, normally having a good front with a deep body and high strong quarters. Its temperament is excellent.

As the title implies, this is a composite breed, but it is so well established and so universally recognized as a breed that it is entitled to a place among the world's breeds of horses. It may be said too, that it has an especial claim to this, because it is composed of the two purest breeds, the Arab and the Thoroughbred, and possesses no alien blood.

The authority in England controlling the breed is the Arab Horse Society, which keeps a Stud Book or Register for the purpose, the conditions of entry being that the Anglo-Arab in question must be: (1) The produce only of Arab horses which are entered either in the Arab Horse Stud Book or the General Stud Book (Arabian Section), and of horses entered in the General Stud Book other than the Arabian Section of the same. (2) Horses directly descended from ancestors which are eligible for entry under the conditions set out at (1) above. (3) Anglo-Arabs bred in foreign countries and entered in the recognized stud books of those countries may also be accepted for registration, if approved by the Council of the Arab Horse Society.

The more usual breeding is by the Arab horse on the Thoroughbred mare, and whether this or the reverse breeding be the case, it can well be understood that the result is a horse of outstanding quality, always supposing that the sire and dam are typical specimens of their respective breeds. It is noticeable, however, that whereas one specimen will be strongly Arab, the other may be markedly Thoroughbred. In the same way as with all breeding, no certainty of height can be looked for, except that the resulting animal will probably be somewhere in height between its sire and dam.

In numberless breed and saddle classes Anglo-Arabs have figured with success in competition with most other breeds of light horses. Because of the added stamina and intelligence derived through the Arab, the Anglo-Arab has proved itself to be a good hunter and a very beautiful hack, having all the necessary gaiety and airiness of movement and the great refinement necessary for this class of animal. It has made its mark in horse trials, flat-races, steeplechases, point-to-point races and in the show-ring, and it is naturally an excellent medium as a dressage horse.

Breed Society (in England): The Arab Horse Society.

In France one differentiates between the 'pure-bred Anglo-Arab' and the 'half-bred Anglo-Arab'. The former is the direct result of cross-breeding with English Thoroughbred (specifically, mares) and pure-bred Arab (specifically, stallions).

The latter springs from two sources: cross-breeding respectively of English Thoroughbred and pure-bred Arab, or of pure-bred Anglo-Arabs with native mares of South-west France.

The present-day Anglo-Arab, long in evolving, has nevertheless kept its original stamp. For many centuries the horse population of the area between the Pyrenees and the Charente passed through varying denominations but retained one characteristic, its original blood, the origins of which go back to the 8th-century Moorish invasion, when stallions from North Africa were used on the mares of Aquitaine. Successively known as the Iberian, Navarrine, Bigourdan and Tarbenian breed, it has now achieved a stable homogeneity under the name of *Race Anglo-Arabe* or *Pur Sang Français*. It has its own Stud Book, only carrying the names of horses with a minimum 25 per cent of Arab blood, and indicating its exact percentage.

The Navarrine breed, highly esteemed for service in the school, was greatly reminiscent of the Andalusian horse, if having greater size and quality. This breed, whose source the wars of the Monarchy, the Revolution and the Empire practically exhausted, received under Napoleon I a strong oriental influx. He greatly appreciated Arab horses and founded two studs, Tarbes and Gélos, where first the Andalusian, then the Syrian horse was cross-bred with native mares. In the 1830s the vogue of racing and therefore of the English Thoroughbred, caused it to be cross-bred with the Navarrine, producing a new type of the latter breed, which came to be called the Bigourdan. Whereas the Navarrine rarely exceeded 15 hands, the Bigourdan was taller (15–16 hands) and longer of line, less well coupled and spindle-legged.

Between 1874 and 1920 timely, well-considered alternate cross-breeding of native mares with English Thoroughbred and pure-bred Arab produced the beautiful breed of the Anglo-Arab Half-bred, also known as the Tarbenian breed. After 1920, successful use was made of Anglo-Arab stallions, thus obtaining a third factor in alternate cross-breeding (English Thoroughbred, Arab and Anglo-Arab). The principal breeding areas are the regions of Tarbes and Pau at the foot of the Pyrenees, and of Limousin, where the Pompadour Stud is the most instrumental of all in the development of the breed.

Today's Anglo-Arab rarely exceeds 16 hands, has a wide forehead, wide-open expressive eyes, longish ears, withers well back, oblique shoulders, a well-muscled, well-oriented arm, a short, well-shaped back, deep chest, low hocks capable of good engagement under the mass, somewhat light but well-boned cannons and sound feet.

The saddle horse *par excellence*, it was used in the 19th century almost exclusively for both light horse cavalry and dragoons. More recently it has often excelled in the Olympic Games, and between the two World Wars its excellent endurance, perfect balance and skill over fences made it a very successful hunter at Pau.

In the origin of this breed we find, as the foundation, a Norman horse which was a powerful and
enduring animal, and very much appreciated in
the early Middle Ages as a war horse.

In later times the Norman horse deteriorated by
careless crossing with the Danish and Mecklenburg
cart-horse, and since 1775 Arabs and English
Thoroughbreds and half-breds were used.   Between 1834–60 a large admixture of Norfolk trotter
blood gave origin to the Anglo-Norman trotter,
which was chiefly bred in the district of Morleraut
(Department of Orne).   The soil of this district is
rich in lime and iron, and in addition to this,
qualities of water and climate favour the breeding
of an excellent horse with good bone and strong
muscles.   Anglo-Norman trotters are very hardy

and enduring and have a very good reputation.

Besides this group of trotters there are two main types of Anglo-Norman: first, the draught type, standing from 15·2 to 17 hands with a strong admixture of Percheron and later of Boulonnais blood, usually grey, but sometimes bay, chestnut or black. The horse was used as a mail-cart horse, thanks to a capacity for pulling a heavy load at a good pace. Secondly, there is the cavalry type, which was much used in the army and for sport. Although some of them are excellent horses, there are many of them which do not answer military requirements and are an unhappy combination of two breeds. Being 'well-topped', their hocks and bone below the knees are sometimes deficient. Good ones, however, make really excellent horses for sport and the now restricted military service. In any event they make good horses for general use.

While the heavier type was bred in the region of Mortagne, Anglo-Norman saddle horses were bred on a large scale around Caen.

This breed, like the other half-breds raised in France, is nowadays known in that country under the name of *Cheval de Selle Français*.

The spotted horse, beloved of the circus and used frequently where a striking appearance together with a docile temperament is required, is to be found in many different parts of the world.   Of recent years commendable efforts have been made in the United States of America to establish and standardize the breed and the Appaloosa Horse Club has been formed there.

The name is derived, it seems, from a breed which was developed by the Nez Percé Indians in the Palouse country of Central Idaho and Eastern Washington, and was produced primarily for war uses.   Something akin to these horses has been found in ancient Chinese paintings dating back over 3,000 years.   A similar type of horse is also known as the Colorado Ranger, for which an authority claims that they are American-bred Moroccan Barbs derived from stock imported from Spanish Andalusia.

The body is pink-skinned and covered by a silky white coat with a large number of black spots superimposed. The spots are of varying sizes and it is a curious fact that they can be felt by a touch of the finger. They are found on all parts of the body and legs, and are in more profusion on the quarters. The effect is very striking and makes them in great demand for circus work. The colouring on many occasions varies both as to the skin and the spots, chocolate often being the colour of the latter.

An infusion of Arab blood has given the horse a touch of quality, and this is particularly noticeable in the refinement of head and gaiety of carriage, making it an animal of considerable attraction not only in appearance but as a riding horse.

In height the Appaloosa may be said to be from 14·2 to 15·2 hands, thus being a handy size for riding, and it weighs, perhaps, 360 to 450 kg (c. 800 to 1,000 lb). Of good shoulder and body, with strong legs having plenty of bone and a well-defined wither, a good specimen conforms to the standard required for riding, and it should be noted that some horses exceed the height given.

It is obviously incorrect to describe all spotted horses as Appaloosas, since this peculiarly marked animal has been known for centuries in various parts of the world. It is for this reason that the British sponsors of the breed describe them as Spotted Horses.

Breed Societies: The Appaloosa Horse Club (of America) and British Spotted Horse Society.

Of all the horse breeds of the world, the Arab is
one of the oldest and one of the most beautiful.
We know that this horse is descended from the
early horse of Central and Western Asia which had
evolved many centuries before the Christian era.

At one time there were many strains of desert
horses and, as far as possible, after the Arab nomads
became possessed of the horse in about the 6th to
7th centuries A.D., breeding from mares was
carefully guarded. In view of the Arab's exceptional
qualities, such as soundness of wind, freedom from
leg trouble, great endurance and the ability to
survive many privations, it is small wonder that
the best of its kind has been greatly cherished and
that some horses have fetched fabulous prices.
Arab stallions have been used to improve many
other breeds of horses and ponies.   But it should

be remembered that the modern westernized
Arabian has now very little in kinship with the
horses of the desert of 200–300 years ago.

The breed's outstanding features are: a small
horse—the stallions standing about 14·2 to 15
hands, with mares slightly smaller—of extremely
graceful carriage and beautifully refined head, with
tail carried high and gaily; a horse of arresting and
picturesque appearance, indeed, the very picture
horse of all the equine race. It is unmistakable
and renowned throughout the world.   It is deeply
regretted that in recent years the breeding of the
Arabian Horse in the desert has ceased to a great
extent, but a number of studs of these beautiful
horses exist in many countries, and the best are to
be found in England.   Today many horses,
among them pure bred Arabs, are to be found in
the U.S.A.

An abbreviated description is given by the late
Lady Wentworth, author of *The Authentic Arabian
Horse* and other books and an authority on the
breed:

Head, small and profile concave, tapering to a
very small muzzle.   Eyes, very large, brilliant and
circular, and placed low in the skull.   Nostrils,
very flexible and capable of enormous expansion.
Jowl, very deep and wide.   Ears, small and
sharply cut, quick and pricked.   Neck, arched and
set into the jaws in an arched curve.   Withers, not
so high, but slope into a strong level back.   Chest,
broad and deep.   Body, well-ribbed-up.   Quarters, broad and level.   Tail, set on a level with the
back and carried high.   Legs, with iron tendons,
large strong hocks, big flat knees, springy pasterns,
well-developed thighs.   Feet, hard and round.
Action, free and fast at all gaits.

Because of its inherent virtues and the increasing demand for the riding horse in England as distinct from the hunter of the last century, the Arab in England has during the last 50 or 60 years increased enormously in popularity; and although the trend of supply and demand varies from time to time, as it always must with any commodity, there is no doubt that the Arab, whether for reproducing the pure breed or for developing the Anglo-Arab or part-bred Arab, will continue to flourish.

This increased demand for the breed is perhaps all the more remarkable because the demand for any horse for army purposes is now practically non-existent. Prior to the 1914 war there was a strong demand for the export of Arab stallions from England to many parts of the world for army purposes, and it would seem now that the demand shows that the Arab has found an entirely new market and thrives there.

Breed Society: Arab Horse Society (of England).

The Ardennes may be considered either as a French or Belgian breed, as the mountains from which it originally came belong according to their exact location to either country.

The Ardennes is a very hardy horse, the most resistant of all to unfavourable conditions of climate and feeding. The breed is very old, and in the last three centuries submitted to many changes, such as increase in size and weight by crossing with Brabants, which was done at the expense of other qualities of the breed, such as power of endurance, vigour and a very good action.

During the 17th century the Ardennes was used as a cavalry horse by Marshal Turenne, and being a good stayer, very hardy, docile, but with a lively temperament, was much appreciated. During Napoleon's campaign against Russia in 1812 Ardennes distinguished themselves, enduring all the hardships much better than other breeds; so did they during the First World War, but then served more as artillery wheelers, as by this time their type was already changed again. Today there exists in the mountains a small Ardennes from 14·2 to 15·1 hands, which is nearest to the old original type, while others are of heavy draught type. The horse is very popular not only in France and Belgium but also in other countries, particularly in Sweden.

Now that the transport in towns and work on farms has become so greatly mechanized, the future of this famous Ardennes breed must, with that of so many others, be largely problematical. But where a working horse of low draught and great hardiness is required, combined with a good free moving gait, the breeding of the Ardennes will continue. No longer, of course, will this horse be required in any quantity for army purposes and it is likely that to a large extent it will be found only in its own country.

The domesticated ass, or donkey, friendly but stubborn, is familiar all over the world, and does not need a long description. There are local variations, but generally it is slaty grey in colour, averaging 10–11 hands in height, with a thick, coarse coat, big head, flat withers, little box-like feet and black dorsal and shoulder stripes. These, forming a cross on the back, are traditionally supposed to date from the first Palm Sunday when an ass carried Christ into Jerusalem. Donkeys are proverbially, and actually, very long-lived.

In India there are two types of domesticated donkey: the small grey, which averages 8 hands and is the usual dark grey with black markings; and the large white, which averages 11 hands.

The wild ass exists in two distinct types, in Africa and Asia respectively. The African ass, the stock from which the domesticated breeds are derived, is very rare, living in small herds in Nubia, Eastern Sudan and Somaliland. Grey, with a white belly, it has large ears and small narrow hoofs and its voice is the familiar bray. Fast and sure-footed, it is much larger than the domesticated 'Neddy'. The onager of Asia (*Equus hemionus onager*) is more horse-like, has smaller ears and is sandy or dun in colour.

One distinct strain, the kiang, is found in the highlands of Tibet. Apart from the general sandy or light chestnut colour, the dorsal stripe and tail tuft are black, while the muzzle, under neck, belly, legs and backs of thighs are creamy-white. The colour becomes darker in the winter, when the coat is long and thick. The kiang is a powerfully built animal ranging in height from 12 to 13 hands, lives in small herds, is very fast for its size and an exceptionally strong swimmer.

Various local strains of *hemionus*, rather smaller and more lightly built, are found in the desert regions of North-west India, Persia (onager), Tartary and Mongolia (dziggetai). The local race of Syria, which must have been the wild ass of the Bible, is now extinct.

So placid is the domesticated African or European donkey, and so friendly in its approach to horses, that it is often turned out with them at grass to exercise a calming influence. In this it is generally successful although attention must be paid to ridding it of lung-worm, to which it is often host.

Description The head of the donkey is short, muzzle small and tapering, the profile concave (dished). The jaws are generous, round and widely open. Ears should be well and firmly set, of good shape and size in proportion to the animal. Within reason, the longer the neck is the better; the top line and under-side to be straight, and the whole should be firm, well fleshed and carried without drooping. The line of back should be practically level and reasonably short. The more oblique the shoulder the better. The ribs should be well sprung and the girth deep. The quarters are long, wide, flat and generously fleshed. The tail is set strong and high. All limbs should be straight and true; knees flat and wide; cannon bones short; hocks set as low as possible. Fore- and hindlegs must not be back-at-the-knee (calf-knee), nor the hindlegs show sickle or turned-in hocks (cow-hocks). Feet should be even and of good shape, hard, clean and smooth of surface, with the typical donkey hoof having a tendency to a low heel. There is no limit to size. For description only, the Society authorizes the use of the following terms (all measurements to be made without shoes):

Miniature an adult donkey below 9 hands.
Small Standard 9 to 10·2 hands.
Large Standard 10·2 to 12 hands.
Spanish Donkey over 12 hands.

Breed Society : The Donkey Show Society.

There are few more famous horses than the
Waler, the national horse of Australia, though it is
not often seen in England.   The term "Waler" is
a comprehensive national term covering a variety
of types, and an abbreviation of New South Wales,
the state where the Australian horse was first imported and bred.

There was no indigenous native horse in Australia, and the first arrivals from the outer world
came in 1795, from the Cape and Chile.   So the
foundation stock of the Waler was of Dutch and
Spanish origin, with the oriental horses the Arab
and the Barb as the ultimate ancestors.   (See also
the note on the Cape Horse under Basuto.)

These original animals were small, and as the
settlers had great need for riding horses and
wanted the best, pure Arab and English Thorough-

bred stallions were imported and used on good mares of riding type. The country, with its equable climate, unlimited range, and wide choice of pasturage, was eminently suitable for horse-breeding, which was carried out with great care; and the Australian horse developed and flourished. It has been asserted, with some justification, that between Waterloo and the Crimean War Australia possessed probably the best saddle horse in the world, and during that period began the supply of cavalry and artillery troop horses to India. Racing, which first appeared in Australia in 1826, further helped to establish the Australian horse, the breeding of which has spread in the natural course of time from New South Wales to the states of Victoria and Queensland; but the name 'Waler' still applied to them all.

The Waler has always been noted for jumping in its own country, high-jumping competitions being a speciality at all shows. Another activity at which it can at times excel is buckjumping, equalling in this respect, in the opinion of many, that better-known exponent, the American bronco. By the same token the Australian range rider takes his place among the world's finest horsemen.

Australian horses are all shapes and sizes, including besides the Waler a draught-horse breed developed from three English strains—Clydesdale, Shire and Suffolk Punch—and the ponies from Western Australia, from stock brought from Timor. This Timor stock must have been representative of the Java horse from the islands of Java and Sumatra.

In Austria-Hungary before the war, besides indigenous and numerous half-bred horses used for
both saddle and harness, there were Austrian
breeds such as the Lipizzaner, Kladruber (above)
and Pinzgauer. The Kladruber horse takes its
name from a place in Bohemia where it was bred at
the Imperial Stud. They are derived from
Spanish horses imported to Austria and Bohemia
from Spain and Italy, and from which they inherited most of their typical characteristics, such
as conformation, high action, roman noses and long,
heavy-crested arched necks. The selection went
in the direction of increasing considerably their
size (they stand 17 to 18 hands) and producing
either black or white animals. With their high
action in teams of six or eight of one colour they
made the most imposing Imperial carriage horses
and were used only on very big occasions. Their

practical value was never taken into much account.

The Pinzgauer, usually roan in colour, is a very powerful, heavy-draught horse standing 15 to 16 hands, and having clean, strong legs. It is said to trace its origin to the Friesian horses and was bred first in the Pinzgau district of Styria. Later on its breeding was extended to Upper Austria and its export organized.

The Pinzgauer is a typical heavy-draught horse of good shape, having an exceptionally good body and satisfactory shoulder for the work required of it. Colour is often roan with dark spots. Short on the leg, it is admirably suited for slow, heavy, direct traction, and as the Percheron is to France, so is the Pinzgauer to Austria. Its future, as with that of other horses required for work as distinct from pleasure, must be problematical.

As with all breeds of heavy or 'cold blood' horses, what these typical Austrian horses lack in activity and intelligence they gain in tractability and docility. Having regard to their strength—and this again applies to all heavy breeds—those who handle them can only be thankful for this placid temperament.

This breed had its native home in Morocco and Algeria, and in its original form stood from 14 to 15 hands in height. It is characterized by flat shoulders, rounded chest, relatively long head, and, as compared with the Arab, the lower setting of the tail, the hair of which, like that of the mane, is profusely developed. The prevailing colours are dark bay, brown, chestnut, black and grey. The skull has the same sinuous profile as that of the Arab. Formerly the Barb was extensively crossed with Syrian Arabs, while later in Algeria it was much mingled with European horses, so that pure-bred animals became very far from easy to obtain. The Barb will thrive on as poor fare as the Arab and is equally hardy in constitution and docile in temper, although somewhat less spirited.

Several strains of the Barb type can be distinguished. The first group was reared by the Mograbins on the western side of the plains south of the Atlas; they called the horse 'Shrubat-ur-rich' (Drinker of the Wind). This horse, which was either grey or brown in colour, was low and greyhound-like in shape, and carried very little flesh. More remarkable is the Bornu breed, from the district south of Lake Chad, which is greyish-white in colour with black legs. The tail is set rather low, the legs and feet are beautifully made and the body is relatively short.

A third breed occurs typically in the Dongola district of Nubia, and is similar to the Bornu. Smaller horses are known in other areas.

Although single specimens are found from time to time, the Barb has for many years now been practically non-existent in England. This is a pity, for there is much that is good about the breed, and its reputation for hardiness is unsurpassed. Its absence is particularly to be regretted as it is essentially a riding-horse, and it is, after all, the riding-horse that will survive in numbers. The reason for its lack of popularity in this country is possibly that it cannot compete in favour with the other great oriental breed, the Arab.

This, however, can be no excuse for the virtual eclipse of the breed outside its native land, for a good Barb would always compare favourably with many breeds of riding-horses and even surpass some of them.

The famous Basuto pony is not in its origin an
indigenous African breed. The horse (*Equus
caballus*) was unknown in South Africa until the
middle of the 17th century, although its ultimate
ancestor was flourishing on the North African
littoral. With the enormous jungles that lay between the north and the south and the belts of the
dreaded tsetse fly, there was little chance of its
migrating southwards by land. The opening of
the sea routes to the East by the Portuguese and
Dutch prepared the way, and in 1653 four horses
of Arab and Barb blood from Java were landed in
the Cape by the Dutch East India Company.

These were the first horses to set foot in South Africa, and they became the foundation of the Cape Horse, which was the direct ancestor of the Basuto Pony.

The importation of oriental strains—Arab, Barb and Persian—continued steadily up to 1811. In the 18th century, when the English began to be interested in the country, the introduction of English Thoroughbred stock began. Between 1770 and 1790 especially, many good English stallions were imported, mainly descendants of 'Herod', 'Matchem' and 'Eclipse', so the Byerley Turk, the Darley Arabian and the Godolphin Barb were all represented, and the oriental ancestry was present on both sides.

The Cape Horse breed flourished during the early years of the 19th century, figured conspicuously in the Boer War and achieved a high reputation for looks and stamina. Then, partly owing to lack of interest and the introduction of inferior foreign stock, the quality of the breed dropped off, deteriorated considerably since 1860, and is now for all practical purposes represented by the Basuto.

The Cape Horse was introduced into Basutoland as a result of border raids and the confusion caused by the invasion of that territory by the Zulus from 1822 onwards. The stolen horses figured in many a conflict, contributing great moral effect on behalf of those who had ventured to ride them. From about 1830 onwards the type developed into the Basuto pony as it is known today: small, thickset, short legs, longish back, very hard hoofs, with that bit of quality about the head which declares its high ancestry. Brought up and worked among the formidable heights of the Drakensberg with no horsemastership or care, but ridden by absolutely fearless riders, the Basuto became as tough and self-reliant as a wild horse and one of the most fearless and surefooted ponies in the world, being habitually ridden at a gallop up and down hills where most other horses and riders would hesitate to walk.   The endurance of these ponies, too, is very great, and they are capable of carrying 82 or 88 kg for 96 to 130 km (13 or 14 stone for c. 60 to 80 miles) a day.   In their own country they became in great demand for racing and polo.

Although Basutos were much used in the Boer War, the breed had already begun to decline, the descent becoming more rapid in the beginning of this century.   Efforts were then started, and are now continuing, to revive the breed by the introduction of good Arab stallions and carrying out breeding on systematic lines.   The experiment of introducing Highland Pony blood was tried in 1917, but the cross was not ultimately successful.

In a country such as South Africa where records seem to show that an increased interest is being taken in the breeding of light horses, where polo flourishes in a smallish way and where riding clubs and pony clubs increase in numbers, the Basuto pony may well stage a come-back.   It may be that the pony will be crossed to the extinction of the true Basuto, but the latter gained for itself such a world-wide reputation for hardiness, surefootedness and ability to thrive on the smallest fare that there are strong hopes that it may survive as a breed where others may unhappily proceed to extinction.

The Bitjug horse was the local native strain of the Veronej or Woronesch province of Russia. At the beginning of the 18th century Peter the Great was responsible for improving the breed by crossing native mares to imported heavier Dutch stallions and subsequently introducing both coaching and trotting blood. Horses of this breed make good working horses, standing around 16 hands high. Their strength, endurance, good action and temperament combined with obedience and docility make them very valuable agricultural horses.

The early history of the Boulonnais (French) breed is of a horse which was bred in that region during the Crusades and was much improved by Arab and Barb stallions brought from the Middle East by the French Crusaders. In the course of ages this breed submitted to certain changes and at one time, before railways were popularized, the Boulonnais existed in the form of a very strong horse with good action and stamina, which enabled it to be used in coaches for fast transport, such as bringing fresh oysters from the sea coast to Paris.

The type enjoyed great fame and was exported to other countries where a strong, fast-moving carriage horse, having endurance, was needed. Some of them were exported before the First World War to Poland, and they appeared to be very useful when crossed with local stock.

Today the Boulonnais is a very heavy-draught horse, standing 16 to 17 hands, quick-growing, with great bone and muscles, and may be used for farm work when it is 2 years old.   At 4–5 years old, being horses of enormous weight and power, they are usually employed in industry in big cities. The Boulonnais are much better movers than would be supposed.   They are black, bay, red roan, blue roan and dappled grey.   Once a type of 'postier' and later an agricultural horse, the Boulonnais today, through selection and very strong feeding, is a heavy-draught horse and is bred in two types: the Abbeville type, which is of medium size, and a large, very heavy Dunkirk type.   Although their name derives from Boulogne, they are bred also in Picardy, Artois, Haute Normandie and in parts of Flanders, where a strong, massive horse is needed for very heavy work.

Among connoisseurs of heavy-draught breeds the opinion prevails that a dash of Boulonnais blood in 'cold-blood' breeds plays the same role as that of the English Thoroughbred in the breeding of saddle horses.

In the Boulonnais France has, with the Dutch Draught (q.v.), the strongest and most impressive draught horse in Europe. It resembles the Percheron (q.v.), not only in type but also largely in colour.   The infusion of Arab blood in years gone by is still noticeable in many specimens of the breed, which for the same reason is claimed to possess a certain elegance in spite of its massive appearance.

Brabant (or Brabançon)

Low-lying areas of Belgium with fertile soil and succulent herbage produced a large, very heavy-draught horse, with great power of traction. The Brabant, as it is called, stands between 16 and 17 hands and has great weight, which increases its tractive ability.   It has a very good temperament and is a willing worker, which characteristics, together with its strong constitution, make it popular.   It was used to a great extent for crossing with the now almost extinct Rhenish horse, while those imported to England had a certain influence on forming the Shire breed.   Brabants are also bred in Russia, in the Gorki province, as pure or grade stock, and some of them are registered in state or district stud books.

Brabants were also used for crossing with the old Belgian mountain breed of Ardennes to increase their size and weight.

Belgium, the Netherlands and the northern parts of France have always been famous for producing heavy draught horses of real worth, so much indeed that their export has always been a very considerable trade. It is small wonder therefore that the Brabant, with its 16 to 17 hands, its great weight and enormous strength, has not only always found a ready market in many parts, but has also proved invaluable for crossing.

When considering the origin of any heavy draught horse from any European country, which also includes England, it may be assumed that in many cases there has been a considerable admixture of the blood of various breeds. Bearing this in mind, it is interesting to note that in spite of this, the breeds themselves, whatever they may be, whether Shire, Clydesdale, Percheron, Ardennes or Brabant, retain the characteristics of the breed itself.

The future of all 'cold-blood' breeds is now in the balance. Their future must be a question of haulage economics, with which is involved the willingness or otherwise of labour to work the hours demanded by the keeping of horses—in short, to provide week-end feeding.

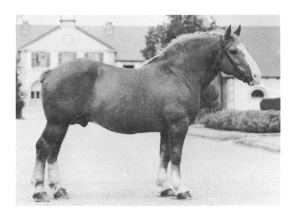

A breed which enjoys in France an excellent reputation, thanks to its great hardiness and working qualities, is the Breton. Bred on the rather poor land of Brittany and exposed to a very rough climate, especially during winter, the Breton makes a very good agricultural horse, being strong and hardy and thriving on poor, indifferent food. There are three distinctive types of Breton horse: heavy-draught horse, Breton draught post horse and Breton mountain draught horse.

The first one is bred on the fertile pastures near the sea coast and represents a type of heavy cart-horse. Those bred in the district of St. Pol de Léon, Côtes du Nord and Finistère stand from 15·2 to 16·2 hands, while the variety of Conquet bred in the south-east of Brest, is about 15·2 hands. They are strong and massive, standing on short legs protected by some feather, and are usually grey or bay.

In the interior of Brittany there is bred a lighter horse, so-called draught post horse, which according to A. Magneville ('Carnet de Notes,' N 2, 1944) is descended from the Norfolk Breton post horse. It stands about 15 to 16 hands, and being not only a strong and hardy horse but also a very good mover, makes a very valuable horse for the farmer.

Besides these two types, there exists a thick-set mountain draught Breton horse which is up to 14·3 hands, and is bred and employed in the mountainous part of Brittany.

As is shown, the Breton horse is to be found in three types which in the main consist of animals of three different sizes—an example, of course, of a country or district breeding the type or types of horses which local requirements demand. This is comparable with the three types or sizes of the Highland pony in Scotland or those three to be found in Wales, the Cob, the Welsh pony of riding type, and the Welsh Mountain pony. The continued existence of the Breton as three types, or indeed its existence at all, must depend upon supply and demand, and it may well be that the smaller or mountain draught horse will be the one which survives.

Horses of the Budyonovsky breed are bred in
studs in the Rostov region of the U.S.S.R. and
have been developed by crossing Don horses (*q.v.*)
with Thoroughbreds.   The result is a horse of
exceptionally good conformation, with a fine front,
good limbs, strong top and well-developed quarters and good hind legs.   It is claimed to have
considerable speed and has a notable record in
steeplechases, Olympic Trials and show-jumping
generally.   The average height is about 16 hands.
The colour is generally chestnut or bay, and in
each can often be found the beautiful golden
shading.

In most of the countries lying to the eastward of the Bay of Bengal, including Burma, Annam (now part of Vietnam), Thailand, the Malay Peninsula and Islands, the Ryukyu Islands and a large portion of China, the horse is represented only by small breeds which come under the designation of ponies. Among these, the Burmese or Shan ponies, which are mainly, if not exclusively, bred by the hill-tribes of the Shan States, in the interior of the country, are believed to be nearly related to the Mongolian breed, although probably modified by the infusion of foreign blood. In stature they are about the equal of the Mongolian and are strong and active, although somewhat slow in their movements. On the other hand, the still smaller but closely allied Manipur (*q.v.*) ponies are much faster, and are used by their owners for polo, of which Manipur is one of the original homes.

The grey-white horses of the Camargue inhabit the remote swampland of the Rhône delta in South-eastern France. Shaggy and wild in appearance, their origin has never been definitely established. The true Camarguais has a wide chest, large barrel, strong quarters and short sturdy legs, and a large, somewhat ugly head with straight or concave profile, the eyes being placed slightly more to the side of the head than in other breeds. Standing only a bare 15 hands but weighing about 362 kg (800 lb), the Camarguais possesses the measurements of a horse of much greater weight.

Camargue horses breed in free-ranging herds on poor reedy pasture, mostly salty marshland. The uneven sparse terrain, particularly bleak in winter and searingly dry and hot in summer, together with the semi-wild life with almost complete lack of man's care, has produced a tough, sure-footed breed with an instinct for survival. Difficult initially to catch and break in, the horses become good agile mounts, able to jump and swim. The *Gardiens*, the cowboys of the Camargue, use the horses for herding the local bulls bred for the native non-lethal *Course Libre*.

For the history of the Camargue horse, see Henry Aubanel's book, *Camarguaises* (1960).

A breed of small pony approximately 11 to 12
hands, found in a limited area between the forested
northern slopes of the Elburz mountains and the
Persian Caspian shores in Northern Iran. It is
unique for its minute size and for its fine strong
bone and shape. It has a head similar to that of the
Arab with large well-placed eyes, short alert ears,
strongly marked jaw, and large low nostrils. It
has well-sprung ribs, tail set high and well carried,
and the hair of both mane and tail fine and silky.
Of a generous and gentle disposition, these ponies
remain apart from the other various breeds in the
area.

Akin to the ponies of Manipur (*q.v.*) are those of Central Sumatra (at one time called Batak or Deli ponies), which used to be exported to Singapore in large numbers. With their handsome, high-bred-looking heads and high-crested necks, they differ markedly, however, from the Mongolian and Yarkandi types, which are often more or less decidedly ewe-necked; this difference being due to a strong infusion of Arab blood. In stature they average only about 11·3 hands, although some reach 12·1 or 12·2 hands. Although most are brown, skewbalds are by no means uncommon. Breeds of ponies are also found in Sumba and Sumbawa; and the Sandalwood pony, with a cross of Arab blood, is also exported.

The Charollais Half-bred is raised mainly in the departments of Loire, Saône-et-Loire, Cher, Allier and Nièvre. Its ancestors were the light little horses of Lorraine, Doubs and Saône, which, crossed alternately with English Thoroughbreds, Norman Half-breds and Vendéens, improved rapidly, turning into a half-bred composite with a strong indigenous strain totally free of hereditary conflicts. Accepted in the past as an excellent cavalry and artillery horse, today it has a good reputation as a hunter.   Like all other types of half-breds, the Charollais has its own stud-book.   If not of the most generous build, it has its ample share of blood and quality.   Standing 15 to 16·2 hands, it is well topped, though a little lacking in the withers, with clean legs and well-shaped feet.   There are few greys to be found in this breed.

The Nivernais and Bourbonnais Half-breds are so similar to the Charollais that they may be considered as one, and consequently all three are known as the *Demi-sang Charollais*; the Limousin and Charollais Half-breds, in turn, are gathered under the denomination of *Demi-sang du Centre*, and, like the other half-breds raised in France, they are also known in that country under the name of *Cheval de Selle Français*.

Claimed as the oldest 'established' breed of English horses, the Cleveland Bay is said to be possessed to an unrivalled extent of the power to transmit to any other breed with which it may be crossed those qualities for which all breeders look, namely, stamina, substance, action, wear and tear with style, appearance and good colour.

The chief use of this horse today is for mating with the Thoroughbred to obtain hunters of quality, up to weight and of good conformation, and for this purpose it is admirably suited. For a long time past it has been exported with great success, chiefly to the United States of America, to grade up to those qualities to which reference has been made horses of inferior breeding.

The breed is of great antiquity and its origin is uncertain, but it may be taken for granted that for a long period of time, in that district of Northern England, and chiefly in the county of Yorkshire, the breed is indigenous. More than 130 years ago the Cleveland must have been the nearest to a fixed type of any race of horses in England, but none the less there were, even then, two types of Cleveland, the one used for agriculture and the other for coaching. It was claimed for the former, and indeed is so still, that it would do all the work of the heavier breeds, that it had the advantage over the Shires and the Clydesdales of being a clean-legged horse (that is, of course, that its heels are devoid of hair), and that it did the work more quickly, being very active. For people in England and other countries it has served well as a ceremonial carriage horse in processions and other displays, and it has always been famous as a coach horse. The whole bay colouring, as the name implies, was suitable and attractive. A team of these bays to a road coach, with their level, striding action, is a sight which must be appreciated by all judges of a good horse.

A general description of the Cleveland Bay is:

Height, 15·3 to 16 hands, on short legs. Colour, bay to bay brown, with only a small white star permissible and a few grey hairs in heels and coronets. Body, wide and deep and not too long, but strong, with muscular loins. Quarters, level powerful, long and oval, with tail springing well away from them. Head, rather large but well carried on a rather long, lean neck. Limbs, strong and muscular with knees and hocks well closed, not less than 23 cm (9 inches) of bone below the knee, the legs clean of superfluous hair, with sloping pasterns.

Breed Society: The Cleveland Bay Horse Society.

The history of the breed of Clydesdale Horses dates from the middle of the 18th century, when the hardy native breed found in the former county, Lanarkshire (now Lanark District, in the Region of Strathclyde) was being graded up to produce greater weight and substance by the use of imported Flemish stallions. The evolution of the breed was the direct result of the efforts of farmers of the Upper Ward of Lanarkshire to meet the demands of commerce, when, following the rapid developments of the surrounding coalfields causing road surfaces to be improved, shoulder haulage was substituted for pack-carrying.

The numbers of the Clydesdale breed seem to have been fairly progressive throughout the period, and in 1877 the Clydesdale Horse Society was formed and almost immediately published its first Stud Book. Since that first publication a very large number of stallions and mares have been registered. The breed has, beyond doubt, proved itself to be very popular and its adherents boast of the great numbers that have been exported as clear evidence of this. Quite spectacular prices have been obtained for big winners in the show ring and for export.

The outstanding characteristics of the Clydesdale are a combination of weight, size and activity, and what is looked for first and last by a Clydesdale man is exceptional wearing qualities of feet and limbs. The former must be round and open with hoof heads wide and springy, for any suspicion of contraction might lead to sidebones or ringbones. To some extent the further requirements of this breed vary somewhat from the orthodox and should be noted. The horse must have action, but not exaggerated, the inside of every shoe being made visible to anyone walking behind. The forelegs must be well under the shoulders, not carried bull-dog fashion—the legs, in fact, must hang straight from shoulder to fetlock joint with no openness at the knee, yet with no inclination to knock. The hind legs must be similar, with the points of the hocks turned inwards rather than outwards, and the pasterns must be long.

The head must have an open forehead, broad across the eyes, the front of the face must be flat, neither dished nor roman, wide muzzle, large nostrils and a bright, clear, intelligent eye. A well-arched and long neck must spring out of an oblique shoulder with high withers; the back should be short with well-sprung ribs; and, as befits a draught horse, the thighs must be packed with muscle and sinew. The colour is bay, brown or black, with much white on face and legs, often running into the body, and it should be noted that chestnuts are rarely seen.

It is interesting to note that of the heavy breeds of horses in the British Isles, any white is strictly forbidden in the Suffolk, is obviously permitted in the case of the grey Percheron, allowed though contested in the Shire, whilst in the Clydesdale it is splashed about in a most generous fashion. White-legged horses are never particularly favoured by the conscientious groom.

It is claimed of the Clydesdales that they are possessed of quality and weight without displaying grossness and bulk, and this is largely true. They are certainly active movers for their size and weight and in consequence are very popular in many cities and on numerous farms, especially in the north of England.

What the future of this breed as an agricultural horse may be is entirely problematical. From time to time those concerned in the breeding of agricultural horses are heartened by statements to the effect that farms are over-mechanized and that prosperity will return to the breeder of agricultural horses and indeed of horses required for town work. But it is only fair to say that no particular evidence of this suggested trend is shown. The Clydesdale in spite of its great size and consequent weight shows perhaps as much quality as, or even more than, any of the heavy breeds and to the lover of the draught horse its extinction would bring great sorrow.

Breed Society: The Clydesdale Society.

As with the hunter and the hack, and, indeed, with certain other well-known English representatives of the horse world, the Riding Cob is not a breed in itself. That it is a type and a well-known one is very certain, and for this reason no work covering the horses and ponies of the world would be complete without a reference to this old-fashioned and still most popular horse.

It will be found that in the majority of the breeds mentioned in this book, other than the pure breeds or horses and ponies indigenous to any particular part of the world, it has been possible to indicate with a fair degree of certainty the components of the particular animal dealt with. This, however, is not even remotely possible in the case of the cob as a type, though, of course, the reverse is so often the case with the individual animal. It is indeed to a considerable extent a chance-bred animal, as will be readily concluded when its general appearance is considered.

The cob may be pictured briefly as a big-bodied, short-legged 'stuffy' horse or pony standing no higher than 15·2 hands, with a small quality head set on a neck arched and elegant. The shoulders are laid obliquely, the back is short and the girth very great. The quarters are generous to a degree and, when viewed from behind, exceed expectations, having second thighs to match. The tail must be carried high, with gaiety, as befits a riding-horse. The action must be close to the ground, not rounded as with the harness horse, and the toe when in action must point to the farthermost limit—to an extent not exceeded, perhaps, in other breeds. The cannon bone should be extremely short.

Cobs are intended primarily for use as hacks, usually heavy-weight hacks for the more elderly rider, and for whatever the purpose, the riding cob must compare favourably, so far as manners are concerned, with that paragon of equine comportment. It is indeed the ideal ride for the elderly and portly, and is called upon to respect in manners and deportment the not-so-very-young.

If it were possible to fix a general line of original breeding no doubt the foundation of many of the best riding cobs has been that from which the Welsh Cob emanated, but equally it is beyond question that many outstandingly successful show-ring cobs have claimed close relationship to half-bred cart mares and heavy-weight hunter mares put to stallions of quality. Whatever the forbears may have been, it is certain that there is nothing more typical nor more easy to recognize than the true Riding Cob. It leaves an unforgettable picture stamped upon the mind.

The Riding Cob has always been popular as a hunter (its great quarters make it outstanding as a performer over fences), as a horse to ride around the farm and as a trainer's hack because of its docility and manners.

The typical cob of the past has always been docked, that is to say the tail has been cut to a length which so-called fashion dictated. Docking, as is known, has been prohibited in various countries for some long while past, and this rule now applies to England, and the prohibition extends to 'nicking,' which is another form of mutilation of the tail.

With or without the full tail, the cob of course remains, and will remain, as a horse up to a very great deal of weight, and its manner must be beyond reproach; it will always be in demand as a riding horse, especially the smaller type which makes mounting easier for the not too agile. With its heavy body and short legs, big barrel and depth through the quarters, there is always a tendency for the cob to be heavy or jarring in its paces, and any suggestion of this of course detracts from its worth as a riding horse, especially for the elderly. Whether the cob of the show ring always conforms to the ideal is a matter of question, and may to some extent be judged by the onlooker. It might be mentioned that a class for cobs at shows is essentially an English institution.

Breed Society: The British Hack and Cob Association.

The term Connemara is applied to the breed of pony which is found in that part of Connaught in Ireland lying to the west of Loughs Corrib and Mask, bounded on the west by the Atlantic and on the south by Galway Bay. This area, which is larger than the actual district of Connemara, has been the home for centuries of an indigenous primitive pony type, which until comparatively recent years was left to fend for itself in an almost feral state in wild and hard conditions.

In 1900 a Commission on Horse Breeding in Ireland was set up, and Professor J. Cossor Ewart, M.D., F.R.S., made a report after a very thorough survey of the conditions and possibilities of the Connemara pony. In 1928 the present Connemara Pony Breeders' Society was formed for the preservation and improvement of the Connemara pony. At its first meeting the Society decided on the policy of maintaining the breed intact by careful breeding from selected Connemara mares and stallions, so as to form a solid foundation stock. The original practice of crossing Connemara mares with stallions of other breeds was discontinued. This policy has been adhered to, and its results are to be found in the increasing uniformity with recognized standards, the better quality generally of mares—owing to the greater attention being paid to this by local breeders—and a decrease in the number of unlicensed stallions at large on mountain commonages and consequently less uncontrolled breeding; while the stamina of the breed, for which it has always been renowned, has not been affected.

As with all the representatives of the various primitive pony breeds of Europe, the origin of the Connemara is lost in the mists of history. It has been said, quite wrongly, that they owe their origin to horses saved from the wrecks of the Spanish Armada in 1588; ponies were, in fact, native to Ireland long before that date. It has been suggested that with the Highland, the Shetland, the Iceland, and the Norwegian ponies (*qq.v.*), it forms a Celtic pony type, with the addition of oriental strains at various times. The breed together with its primitive characteristics certainly shows signs of the admixture of Spanish and Arab blood, and might well have received the former in the times when the merchants of Galway traded regularly with Spain. However that may be, there seems no doubt that the Connemara pony is among the oldest inhabitants of the British Isles, and is a link with a very remote past.

The points and characteristics of the Connemara pony as defined in the Stud Book are as follows: hardiness of constitution, staying power, docility, intelligence and soundness. Height, 13 to 14 hands. Colour, grey, black, bay, brown, dun, with occasional roans and chestnuts. Body, compact, deep, standing on short legs and covering a lot of ground. Riding shoulders (*i.e.*, well sloped and not thick and heavy). Well-balanced head and neck, and a free, easy action and true movement. Bone, clean hard and flat, measuring 17·7 to 20·3 cm (7 to 8 inches) below the knee.

The predominant colour is grey, found in more than half the total number of ponies registered. Blacks are a little more numerous than browns and bays. Dun, the typical and original colour of the Connemara, is now very scarce.

As has been shown, the breed of Connemara Pony is without question an ancient one, and there can be little doubt that the pony as found in Connemara itself is a tough, wiry and altogether typical native pony. Like all such, it thrives on poor keep and, as with other native breeds, seems to do better and retain its type better this way than if stable-fed. It is to be hoped that the true Connemara type will be jealously guarded and retained.

The English Connemara Pony Society now recognize a height limit of 14·2 hands. This recognition curbs the natural tendency of breeders to increase the size, which generally means loss of character. It is indeed essential to retain the true characteristics which are exemplified in the Irish-bred pony.

Breed Societies: Connemara Pony Breeders' Society and English Connemara Pony Society.

The Criollo is the native pony from South America, derived from the original Arab and Barb strains brought to South America through Spain at the time of the Conquest. Having suffered rigorous natural selection covering a period of some three hundred years of wild life, their chief characteristics and qualities of great hardiness and ability to live under exposure have been attained.

At the time of the invasion, the Spanish cavalry ranked as the highest to be found in Europe. In the formation of the Criollo, the oriental blood brought by the Moors to Spain was more potent than that of the horses existing in the Iberian Peninsula, by reason of its greater purity and selection, which lasted through eight centuries of Mohammedan domination, and in consequence, it may be assumed, had considerable influence on the conquest of the New World.

In the South American pampas, driven into a wild environment following the destruction of Buenos Aires by the Indians, new natural selection began to take place, resulting in much physical improvement due to the severe struggle for existence. The weak and organically unsound perished, while the survivors became the progenitors of the Criollo breed. Such formidable disadvantages as prairie fires, great changes of temperature, dust storms, frosts and floods (not to mention wild dogs) had to be contended with. No doubt it is to the advantage of the horse that it has acquired the peculiarly helpful and characteristic dun colouring which is similar to that of the sandy wastes, straw, or burnt-up pastures or gravel of the countryside. In short, the Criollo adopts protective colouring, as do many other animals and plants in nature.

It is small wonder that the breed is outstanding in those virtues which are so necessary to the real utility horse. The Criollo has figured largely and successfully in many endurance tests, both official and otherwise. It may be noted here that the two famous horses 'Mancha' and 'Gato' were Criollos, and that they, at the ages of 15 and 16, took part in that epic of endurance when they carried Professor A. F. Tschiffely from Buenos Aires to New York, overcoming incredible difficulties and covering 21485 km (13,350 miles) at an average of 42·5 km (26·5 miles) on each day's journey, and achieving a record in altitude of 5857 m (19,250 feet). On this amazing journey they travelled 150 km (93 miles) across a desert in Ecuador without water in a temperature of 48·9°C.

Description Dun, bay, brown, skewbald or piebald. Medium-sized. Weight, about 426 kg (940 lb). Height, 13·3 to 14·3 hands. Head, broad at base, poll narrow, broad forehead with plenty of skull, but narrow face. Neck, of medium size. Withers, muscular and clearly defined. Shoulders, semi-oblique. Generous ribs, showing little light under body. Back, short and deep. Croup, semi-oblique. Forearms and legs, broad and muscular. Cannon-bone short with tendons well separated. Joints clean and rounded. Chestnuts small and only in the region of the hocks. Pasterns medium length. Character and disposition, bright and active.

The illustration shows a very ideal type of animal, short legs, a good shoulder, wonderful middle and quarters, a very good length of rein, and altogether a very pleasant horse to look at. No one who has seen and closely studied photographs of 'Mancha' and 'Gato' would suggest that they have any great resemblance to the animal shown here. They are in fact more true to the real type, which is essentially a very hard-working horse. On the other hand, they claim the clean, hard legs, the strong and fine body and good quarters of the horse illustrated. Having regard to the work which this horse has been called upon to carry out in the past, and is in fact now doing in great numbers in South America, it is not surprising that it has an admirable framework on the best of legs.

In Brazil the Crioulo is a smaller horse by some 5 cm (2 inches) than the Argentine Criollo.

Breed Society: Registered in the Argentine Stud Book.

This pony is a native of the North of England, and has inhabited its eastern side from time immemorial. A backbone known as the Pennine Range runs roughly from north to south and from the west came the Fell Pony, while from the east came the Dales. Originally, the two were identical in type and indistinguishable except territorially— the one was the same as the other except in name. Now, the Dales is the larger of the two by perhaps 5 cm (2 inches), and it is of more stocky build.

The Dales Pony was always a weight-carrying type, and for generations in the last century was used for carrying lead from the mines in Northumberland and Durham to the docks in convoys. The ponies were not led, but walked in orderly fashion, controlled by a rider. The weight carried was very great (in all about 100 kg or 16 st) on either side of the body, and the weekly distance was 386 km (240 miles)—a notable feat. To this, no doubt, must be attributed their soundness and that they are free and active workers.

To meet the calls of the market, the modern Dales have lost much of their mountain and moorland character, and indeed it is doubtful whether they can be claimed as such. They make, however, a fine type, and a few of the true type do still exist, but they are largely now a cross-bred.

A description of the true Dales pony may be given as follows. They stand up to 14·2 hands and many are jet black, other prevailing colours being bay, brown and occasionally grey, while chestnuts, piebalds and skewbalds are never seen. They are possessed of much fine hair on their heels, which is counted as important. Action is very good, the feet being put down straight and true, though it is not a rare occurrence for some to go wide behind.

The head is neat and pony-like, with small ears neatly set, and with a fine jaw and throat. The neck tends to shortness with shoulders too steep and straight. Back, loins and hind-quarters are all that can be desired, being ample, strong and full, and the ribs are well-sprung. The tail is not set high as in some of the mountain and moorland breeds.

The feet, legs and joints are all very good, and so too are the knees and hocks, and for its size the pony displays great bone. The whole appearance of the pony gives the impression of exceptional strength in relation to its size. The breed is very largely free from hereditary unsoundness, and in view of the climatic conditions offered by the country, it is naturally extremely hardy. It is claimed of the pony that it is easily broken and will do all the work required on a small farm. Though, of course, subject to market variations, the Dales is a pony which fetches a good price, on account of its extreme utility.

It may be noted here that the working pony for agriculture has never been in great demand in England, certainly not to the same extent as it has been in many other parts of Europe, notably in Scandinavian countries. In Scotland, however, there has been a considerable call for such, especially from the crofters on the small farms and holdings in the innumerable islands and on the mainland. With its docility, activity, strength and general hardiness, the Dales Pony is hard to beat for this purpose.

The future of the Dales Pony must to a large extent depend upon the demand or lack of it for the working pony between the shafts. It may be that in many of the larger towns of England and Scotland there will be a demand for such by the small tradesmen and local hill farmers, and while that demand lasts the Dales should find a place. It is sufficient to look at the illustration shown here, without even looking closely at the detailed description, to realise that the pony is also admirably built for the smallholder or farmer, but, like all horses and ponies which in the past have found their market as working animals, as distinct from those acquired for pleasure, its future can hardly be said to be assured.

Breed Society: The Dales Pony Society.

The indigenous Danish horse was a small, thick-set animal, which later on was crossed with Dutch, Spanish, Turkish and English Thoroughbred blood. Thus were created Danish breeds such as the Frederiksborg, the name of which was taken from the place near Copenhagen, where a great stud existed from 1562 to 1862. There was also the Jutland breed, which was a strong cart-horse very much resembling the Schleswig (*q.v.*). The province of Schleswig, which at one time belonged to Denmark, was a great asset in Danish horse-breeding. In some coast districts and on certain of the islands there is still seen a sturdy pony much resembling the ponies of Sweden and Finland. To the same group belongs the Iceland Pony (*q.v.*).

This is the third principal Bulgarian breed, based on the Nonius breed (*q.v.*) of the G. Dimitrov Stud Farm. The Danubian horses are of medium size, massive but compact, with energetic movements. The average height is 15·2 hands.

The Danubian is a good performer for a medium heavy load and for equestrian events, especially jumping, and is used as foundation stock for the improvement of the horse population in Northern Bulgaria along the banks of the Danube river, and in the plains of Southern Bulgaria.

Special measures have been taken for the development of these horses over the past 20 or 25 years. The foundation stock includes at present 100 English Thoroughbred mares and 16 stallions, mostly imported from U.S.S.R., Poland, the German Democratic Republic and Rumania.

The rugged waste of Dartmoor, in the extreme
south-west of England, with its grim and towering
tors, its rock-strewn slopes and forbidding bogs—
offering at best but the poorest feed, would hardly
commend itself to the uninformed as a suitable
ground for feeding ponies; yet here are bred the
famous Dartmoor ponies.   Here for centuries unknown the Dartmoor has lived and multiplied,
while watchful and wise Nature has seen to it that
only the fittest survived.   Thus it happens that, in
common with the other mountain and moorland
breeds of the British Isles, a pony, quite indigenous
and quite distinctive, roams this bleak countryside
in a practically wild state, breeding and, literally,
when the land is mantled in snow, scratching for an
existence.   These ponies remain entirely un-

handled unless rounded-up for sale, and few of the mares and still fewer stallions ever have a hand laid on them except for branding purposes.

Essentially a riding-pony, the Dartmoor, if handled young, makes as good a riding-pony as can be found, and in size and conformation is much akin to its neighbour the Exmoor, both of which breeds can make a long-honoured claim to be good ponies for the young. Nevertheless, in spite of their small size, they are up to a surprising amount of weight; yet fashion and a misguided prejudice decrees that as soon as a child grows any length of leg, a pony inches higher must be procured.

The Dartmoor is a good-looking pony, compact, the best of them conforming well to the accepted standard of any riding-horse or pony, being possessed also of a certain elegance which is very pleasing. It is long-lived, and will see a big family of children through from oldest to youngest and then give good service when passed on to another household. As with all the mountain and moorland breeds of the British Isles, the pure-bred Dartmoor is invaluable as foundation stock, as the records of many of them have shown times without number. Bred up from these excellent foundation ponies, as well as from the Exmoor and Welsh mountain ponies, hunters, hacks and children's ponies have appeared as prizewinners on countless occasions and at the most important shows throughout the length and breadth of the British Isles.

Description Height, not exceeding 12·2 hands. Colour, bay, black or brown preferred, but no colour bar except Skewbalds and Piebalds. Excessive white to be discouraged. Head should be small, well set on and blood-like. Ears, very small and alert. Neck, strong, but not too heavy, and neither long nor short—Stallions, moderate crest. Back, loins and hindquarters, strong and well covered with muscle. Feet, tough and well shaped. Action, low, free, typical hack or riding action. Tail, set high and full.

For some long while past breeders of the true Dartmoor Pony have suffered a period of great anxiety. Up to perhaps the early days of the present century the habitat of the pony was roamed by the true Dartmoor Pony. To meet the need for very small ponies to work in the mines, certain moormen, without regard to the retention of the pure breed, introduced Shetland stallions indiscriminately to the moors, with the result that the Dartmoor-Shetland cross obtained a very strong footing, and as such cross-breeding was carried out in a very haphazard way many small ponies of most indifferent, and sometimes degenerate, type, multiplied to the exclusion of the true Dartmoor.

The Dartmoor Pony Society, The British Horse Society and others have made strenuous but not altogether successful efforts to remove this trouble. It is to the credit of the Society and a few individual breeders that they have in small numbers retained the purity of the breed. It is now bred in considerable numbers outside the confines of Dartmoor.

Breed Society: The Dartmoor Pony Society.

This well-known breed makes a high-class saddle
horse.   It is bred in the districts of the Don and
Volga rivers.   Originally it was a small horse, but
its size was increased and the conformation improved by introduction of Karabakh and later of
Thoroughbred blood.   The amazing powers of
endurance of the Don horses are almost unbelievable.   It was with these tough horses that
the Cossacks harrassed Napoleon's ill-fated army
in 1812, subsequently marching on Paris and back
to Russia again, a feat unequalled in cavalry history.
The favourite golden colour is inherited from the
Karabakh.   Height is 15·1 to 15·3 hands.

The Dutch Draught Horse belongs to the most massively built and most heavily muscled breeds of Europe. The official descent can be traced back to the second half of the last century by means of the Stud Books of the Royal Netherlands Draught Horse Society, which covers the whole of the country and includes all Dutch Draught Horse breeders, its aim being the improvement and promotion of Draught Horses in the Netherlands.

In order to consolidate the characteristics of the breed, no horses of unknown pedigree have since 1925 been entered in its Stud Book, and this is the only one in the Netherlands based upon absolutely pure breeding, since only the progeny of officially registered parents is made eligible for entry. Horses are not entered until their pedigree has been carefully checked and an accurate description has been supplied. When a registered horse is over two and a half years, it can be entered in the Preferential Stud Book, after passing a special examination of its conformation. For an even further grading of Preferential mares and stallions, inter-provincial prize examinations are held at regular intervals, and once a year a National Show is held, at which not only conformation but also breeding achievements and pedigree are judged.

Draught Horse breeding in the Netherlands has developed rapidly and has been pursued in all provinces for many decades, and is now very successfully carried on throughout the country, on all types of soil, including sandy, peaty and heavy silty soils. Today the breed is recognized as being docile under all circumstances, willing, active, with a pleasant, courageous disposition. It is famous for its exceptionally long working life—it can be used for light work on the farm at two years or even under—for its durability, great fecundity and excellent breeding performance. It has a quiet and intelligent temperament and great stamina. Last, but not least, it is very moderate in its feeding requirements and can be successfully maintained on plain fare.

Description The Dutch Draught Horse is a massive, hard, deep animal of heavy build. The neck is very short, carrying a not too heavy head, with withers little developed and shoulders more often than not heavily loaded. The legs are well-placed, correctly shaped and heavily muscled, with good feet; the fore-quarters are well developed and massive, the back strong and wide with well-sprung ribs, and the hind-quarters wide, heavy and powerful. The tail is low-set, the croup sloping more perhaps than in any other breed. Colour bay, chestnut or grey: black rarely seen.

Selection work on the breed began on the Kabiuk
Farm in the late 19th century, with a stud of
Anglo-Arabs, cross-bred English mares from
Poland and from Bulgarian state farms, and native
and Arabian mares. Improvements were first
made through English Thoroughbred or cross-bred
sires (out-breeding), then through line-breeding.
In 1951 the Ministry of Agriculture took over the
Military Stud Farm Bozhurishte, and created a
foundation stock the S. Karadja State Farm near
Balchik. The Bozhurishte horse has a close genetic
link with the English cross-bred of the V. Kolarov
State Farm and with the East Bulgarian strain; the
Kolarov and Karadja stock is almost identical.
Average height is 16 hands.

The Exmoor pony is the descendant of the native British wild horse and is believed to be an indigenous animal that has been preserved in its aboriginal state from the earliest times to the present day. This apparently is borne out by the research work which has been done in the department of anatomy in the Royal (Dick) Veterinary College, Edinburgh.

The large tract of wild country known as Exmoor lies in the South-west of England and is contained in the extreme west of the county of Somerset, though some adjacent moors lie in the county of Devon. It is a wild part for England, sparsely inhabited, and the ponies run wild over a series of high, bleak moorlands. Although the 'keep' is of a better quality than that to be found in the New Forest, they have a hard life in winter and they can claim, because of this and the survival of the fittest, to rank with the other mountain and moorland breeds for stamina and naturally acquire that characteristic sure-footedness common to these groups of native ponies.

The true and pure native Exmoor owes much to Sir Thomas Acland (d. 1871) and his family, which consistently maintained the old type of pony. As with all other of England's native pony breeds, its origin is obscure and of great antiquity. Historians seem to agree that it is strictly indigenous and probably as old as the first inhabitant.

Experiments have been made from time to time, as with the other native breeds, to increase the size of the pony by the introduction of alien blood, but the attempts met with varying success. Lovely ponies have been bred, but these do not stand up to the rigours of the wild winter storms.

The true-bred pony roaming the moors remains small, hardy and true to type. Let anyone see these mealy-nosed ponies, living on grass, probably never having tasted corn in their lives, carrying full-grown men through a long day with the Devon and Somerset Stag Hounds up to the finish; let him ponder for a moment on the animals' strength, courage, speed and endurance, and he will not be surprised that the merit of the breed has been discovered and appreciated.

Large numbers of these ponies have been seen in England, not only in harness but more particularly as children's riding-ponies. They are rather wild in coming to hand, but if taken off the moor young enough and handled with care and consideration, they make good and lovable mounts for young people, and give honest service through a long life. Their outstanding characteristic is that they all have a mealy nose or muzzle and show no white markings whatsoever. When seen at the National Pony Society's Annual Breed Show in London, the Exmoor has compared favourably with the other breeds of mountain and moorland ponies, and has done well in the classes under saddle. Many a young one bought in the rough at the annual sale at Bampton, in Devon, has taught several in a family to ride.

Description General appearance or type, definite 'pony' character, hard and strong, vigorous and alert and symmetrical in appearance. Head and neck, ears short, thick and pointed, clean-cut face, wide forehead, eyes large, wide apart and prominent (toad eyes), wide nostrils, mealy muzzle, clean throat, good length of rein. Shoulders, clean, fine at top, well laid back. Chest, deep and wide between and behind forelegs. Ribs, long, deep and well-sprung and wide apart. Back, broad and level across loins. Tail, neatly set in. Legs, clean and short, with neat hard feet, forelegs straight, well apart and squarely set, hind legs well apart, nearly perpendicular from hock to fetlock with point of hock in line with pelvic bone, wide curve from flank to hock joint; legs free in motion with no tendency to sweep or turn. Action, straight and smooth. Coat, close, hard and bright in summer. Colour, bay, brown or dun, with black points, mealy colour on muzzle, round eyes and inside flanks, no white markings. Quality, alert expression and general poise indicating balance and symmetry of movement, fine clean bone. Height, stallions 4 years and over, not exceeding 12·3 hands, mares 12·2 hands.

Breed Society : The Exmoor Pony Society.

Falabella (Miniature)

This breed of miniature horse has been developed during the last 100 years in the Argentine by the Falabella family on the Recreo de Roca Ranch, outside Buenos Aires. Their height does not exceed 76 cm (30 inches) at maturity, so they can claim to be the world's smallest horse. The Shetland pony was the basis of the breed, which was developed downwards by in-breeding and crossing with the smallest possible animals. Unfortunately no records have been kept. The breed appears to be stabilized at the present size, and they are much in demand in North America as pets and for use in harness. All colours are found, but Appaloosa-marked ones are being specially bred.

Upwards of 60 years ago the Fell Pony was used
to carry the lead from the mines to the docks on
Tyneside, in Northern England. Moving freely
and in droves of twenty, these ponies carried
100 kg (16 st) of lead, pannier fashion, 50 kg (8 st)
a side. In the charge of a mounted man, this
drove was kept together at a steady walk, and
386 km (240 miles) per week was the pony's
job. These were the Dales and Fell ponies. In
those days there was no distinction between the
breeds.

 The Pennine Range of hills is the backbone running down the North of England separating
Cumbria from Northumberland, Durham and
Yorkshire. It is a great range of wild moorland,
with but few scattered farms, where only the
hardiest animals can stand the climate. Roughly,
from the crown of the hills away to the west and

in the mountains of Cumbria, overshadowing Windermere, Ullswater, Derwentwater and the lesser lakes, the Fell ponies are to be found running wild, and finding what they can to sustain life on these precipitous and none-too-hospitable hills. On the other side, away to the east, is the home of the Dales pony—the brother breed—a rather more stocky pony and standing a little higher.

Although formerly used as a pack pony, carrying great weight, the Fell pony is an excellent riding-pony; indeed, as a general utility ride-and-drive, it is hard to beat.   From the admirable show type seen at the Ponies of Britain Annual Show held at Ascot, to the rough and rather uncouth animal seen in its native surroundings, the Fell seems to breed wonderfully true to type; indeed, of all the mountain and moorland breeds of Britain, none breeds more truly to type than the Fell.

Description Height not exceeding 14 hands. Colour, black, brown, bay or grey. Head is small with a broad forehead, tapering to the nose. The neck is of proportionate length, giving good length of rein. The stallion has a moderate crest. Shoulders are well laid back and sloping, not too fine at withers or loaded at point; good, long, shoulder blade and well-developed muscles. The back is strong and the loins muscular. The car-case is deep, thick through the heart, round ribbed, short and well coupled. Hind-quarters are square and strong; tail is well set on. Feet are of good size, round, open at heels. Pasterns are fair, slop-ing but not too long. Forelegs are straight and big with well-formed knees; short cannon bone and plenty of good bone below knees, 20 cm (8 inches) at least; great muscularity of arm. Hindlegs have good thighs; hocks well let down and clean cut;

plenty of bone below joint; plenty of fine hair (coarse hair objectionable) at heels; all except at point of heel may be cast in summer. The pony should have a smart and true walk and a well-balanced trot with good knee and hock action, going well from the shoulder and flexing the hock; should show great pace and endurance. The Fell is constitutionally as hard as iron with good pony character, an alert and lively appearance and great bone.

Reference has been made to the alliance of the Fell with the Dales Pony, and although there is now some difference in height and a very considerable difference in appearance (as will be seen from the illustrations under both breeds) the fact remains that they were at one time practically identical, the difference in name being purely territorial. A great change, however, now separates the two, and this has been brought about by cross-breeding, and by the introduction of heavy horse blood. The Fell Pony Society and the pony's breeders are very jealous of the purity of the breed and are unlikely to permit the introduction of any alien blood. Of all our mountain and moorland breeds there are few more easily recognized than the black or brown Fell Pony, with its very long and full mane and tail and, for a pony, generously feathered heels.

Breed Society: The Fell Pony Society.

Another breed of Belgian horses is the Flemish,
which is said to be closely related to the Friesian.
England used to import a great number of Flemish
horses from the time of Richard I. Documents
prove that at least 100 stallions, including many
Brabants, were imported into the country, so that
many of our heavy horse breeds carry a considerable
amount of Flemish and Brabant (or Brabançon)
lines.

Belgium has always had a preference for heavy
horses, and from the 11th century until the 16th
century, Flanders and Brabant were the centres for
the studs of the Great Horse. Dutch, Holstein
and Danish horses were introduced into the studs
in the 17th and 18th centuries, and in the second
half of the 19th century a great demand for heavy
horses had to be met. Because this demand has
fallen off in the 20th century, the Flemish horse is
now fighting a battle against extinction.

It is estimated that 90 per cent of Belgium's
horses are of the 'cold-blood' type. The oldest
'blood line' is 'Orange I' (1863–1885), whose
descendants are 'Jupiter' and 'Brilliant', and
especially 'Albion d'Hor', whose blood is found in
almost every pedigree of these heavy horses. Only
ten to twelve mares are accepted for each stallion.
Horses are exhibited annually at the Brussels show.

Though the French had been importing English Thoroughbreds from the late 18th century, the French breed was not made official until the 1830s. Breeders, in emphasizing staying power, made their racehorses amongst the best in the world. 'Monarque', the first truly great thoroughbred, founded one most successful French blood line. Other influential sires were the grey 'Le Sancy'; 'Dollar'; 'St Simon'; 'Galopin'; and 'Brantôme'.

Races were at first restricted to horses bred and raised in France, but in 1863 the Grand Prix de Paris, an international race, was founded on the initiative of the Duc de Morny. Two years later, when 'Gladiateur' won the British Triple Crown, French Thoroughbreds began to gain substantial recognition outside France. The revival of French Thoroughbred racing after the Second World War was largely due to M. Marcel Boussac, at whose Fresnay-le-Buffard Stud 'Tourbillon', by 'Ksar', and 'Pharis', by 'Charos', produced many outstanding racehorses. Baron Guy de Rothschild at Méautry, Mme Volterra, Jean Stern, François Dupré and Prince Aly Khan also made important contributions. French Thoroughbreds are noted for their staying power.

Thoroughbred breeding has been mainly concentrated in Normandy and the Paris region. While most are bred for racing, Thoroughbreds are also used on brood mares of various local breeds in an effort to upgrade them generally, because a Thoroughbred invariably provides the necessary stimulus, more particularly for all forms of competition. The Thoroughbred as a breed is now standard throughout the world, and the French horse is similar to one of English breeding (see Thoroughbred).

This breed, one of the oldest in Europe, is entirely indigenous to the Netherlands, and as it is found today its production is limited in the main to the province of Friesland, where it is claimed that it is bred with increasing success in the so-called meadow districts and in sandy soil areas. Its popularity is said to be largely based on the admirable character of the horse, for it excels in docility, willingness and cheerful temperament, enabling unskilled labourers to handle the horse without risk. It is, furthermore, an economical feeder and will keep its condition on rations which would mean starvation to some breeds.

A finely chiselled head with small ears is carried on a shapely neck with an exceptionally long mane, which has been known to reach the ground. The back is strong, and ribs deep and well-rounded, though the tail, which carries much hair, is set rather low. The legs also are heavily covered with hair, sometimes right up to the knee joint, and it should be noted that the colour is always black, though a small star is occasionally met with. Neither docking nor trimming of the mane or tail is tolerated in the Friesian horse, and would bar registration in the Friesian Stud Book, which was founded in 1879.

Prior to being entered in the Stud Book, the stallions and mares have to comply with high standards of conformation and pedigree, purity of breed being of major importance. After a special examination they are submitted to a strict veterinary inspection.

During the years of the Second World War breeding activities greatly increased, since in this period all sorts of difficulties were put in the way of mechanized traction. The efficient management of the Stud Books and the excellent breeding material available made it possible to create a large horse population of a quality even better than before. Because of its impressive colour, its tractability and natural, balanced carriage, the Friesian stallion has of late become popular as a circus horse, and it is claimed that the demand is ever increasing. As a nation the Dutch have always been very attracted to the harness horse in the show ring, and it is a frequent and popular spectacle to see in the ring Friesian horses drawing Friesian gigs, the occupants being, perhaps, a gentleman with his lady, both in the old Friesian costume, while to complete the picture the Friesian National Anthem is played. Height about 15 hands.

It is claimed for this breed, which is a native of Mexico, that it originated in Galicia in North-west Spain and was among those which were bred by Cortés when he landed in South America.

Description The height is from 12 to 13·2 hands at maturity and the weight from 272 to 317 kg (600 to 700 lb). Solid colours prevail, the majority being bays, blacks, sorrels and a few duns. No paints, pintos or albinos are eligible for registration. The Galiceño is extremely gentle and easy to handle. Its good disposition, even after a hard ride or workout, is another reason why it makes an ideal 'all family' horse. It is bright and alert, and very quick to learn, high intelligence being a fundamental trait. For hundreds of years the Galiceño has been used for pulling carts, carrying pack supplies and doing ranch work, as well as acting as an excellent riding animal. Although small, the Galiceño is remarkably hardy with an abundance of natural courage and stamina.

The Galiceño has now been imported into the United States of America.

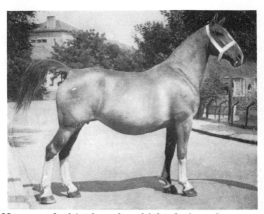

Horses of this breed, which derives its name from the Dutch province of Gelderland, where breeding is still carried on quite extensively, originate from a very old native breed which was crossed many years ago with such stallions as English Thoroughbreds, Norfolk Trotters, Holsteins and Anglo-Normans. During the past decades, the main consideration has been consolidation of type, with very remarkable results, for the breed has greatly improved of recent years, the modern horse being wide and deep, yet of beautiful build, with a very stylish action. A docile farm horse and an excellent saddle-horse, it is claimed to be an unsurpassable show horse in the Netherlands. In the past, several Royal Studs, including Great Britain's, have been regular buyers of these horses. Height ranges from 15·2 to 16 hands, although larger animals are occasionally met with.

A Hungarian breed, the Gidran, larger than the Shagya, was formed by crossing native mares with English Thoroughbred and English half-bred stallions. The Gidran is a big saddle-horse, standing about 16 hands, with a beautiful characteristic head and good conformation, and is usually chestnut or brown in colour. It has a great capacity for galloping and is a comfortable and good-looking cavalry horse. Its breeding is very popular not only in Hungary but also in other countries. In Poland in particular, Prince Sanguszko's stud at Gumniska produced a very useful horse, deep in body with typical conformation.

Better known, perhaps, than the Gidran, is the Hungarian breed Nonius, which owes its name to the Anglo-Norman stallion of that name. This horse was used as a sire with great success and is considered as the founder of the breed. There are two well-recognized types of this breed: the Large Nonius and the Small Nonius. The first type is a rather massive, big-boned animal, standing very often 17 hands, while the Small Nonius is much lighter in type and general appearance and stands about 15·2 hands. Both these varieties, however, are not genetically bred as such, but they come out in breeding; one may, indeed, have Large and Small Nonius sometimes from the same mare. The Nonius has a very quiet disposition, excellent action, and makes a very good horse for both agricultural and military purposes; the Large Nonius made a good horse-artillery wheeler. It is recognized as a drawback to this breed that they are not hard enough. Their usual colour is dark bay.

The Gothland Pony is claimed as the oldest breed in Scandinavia and one that is relatively free from alien blood. As with so many other ancient breeds its ancestry in many respects is open to doubt, although it is probably descended from the wild Tarpan. In more modern times Arab blood was introduced, but even this was many years ago. The breed has enjoyed much popularity over a long period, but has also, at times, been less in fashion.

Following a marked decrease in the numbers of the breed at the beginning of the 20th century, when the general quality, however, showed a marked improvement, successful and more controlled breeding seems now to be taking place.

Today the following is a fair description of the Gothland Pony. It is a small, rather light and elegant pony, which is gentle and easily handled. It has a small head with broad forehead, small pricked ears, big expressive eyes, big nostrils, with a firm mouth. The neck is short and muscular with long sloping shoulders; the back is on the long side; croup round and short. The legs, though light of bone, are strong and well covered with muscle, while the hoofs are small, hard and of good shape. The height is 12 to 12·2 hands. All colours including Duns and Palominos.

Essentially a Dutch farm horse, the Groningen can be used successfully as a heavy-weight saddle-horse and is also an excellent carriage horse, showing speedy, responsive and stylish action, with much natural bearing and great endurance. Of good conformation, this horse has a strong back and deep body, with legs and feet of excellent substance, and a very refined head and neck, yet thrives on poorish fare. Its strongest characteristics are said to be docility and obedience. Height ranges from 15·2 to 16 hands, although larger specimens are permitted. Despite a comparatively heavy weight, the horse is primarily a light draught horse, of pure breed and good pedigree.

The photograph is of the Gudbransdal pony of Norway, which is similar to the Fell pony of Britain. It is generally black or brown in colour. The breed evolved from heavy Danish horses, with crosses of Thoroughbred and Trotter blood. The dun Norwegian Fjord Pony is better known and can be seen in harness classes in Britain.

The name 'hack' is essentially British and is of quite ancient origin, but it must not be confused with the word "hackney," for in modern times the latter indicates the harness-horse, while the hack denotes the refined riding-horse. Furthermore it should be noted that the hack is in no sense an established breed, but as it is most definitely a type it has its place in this book.

The hack in Britain is any horse or pony which is suitable for riding, but for the purposes of this short note it is desirable to treat it according to the standards laid down by the British Hack and Cob Society, which decrees that it must not exceed in height 15·3 hands, and not being an established breed it can be of any colour.

To win in the show-rings of the United Kingdom or Ireland, any horse conforming to the height and having the necessary quality and manners may be of any breed or any admixture of breeds, but in practice, as extreme refinement and performance are the principal factors, it follows that the winner is usually found in the Thoroughbred. All, therefore, that is expected in the Thoroughbred of great quality (and it should be noted many Thoroughbreds fail considerably in this respect) is needed in the winning hack. Indeed, those points, such as the refined head to fit the neck of true proportions, the well-laid-back shoulder, the pronounced, though not exaggerated wither, short back with big girth and well-sprung ribs and powerful quarters, must be found, if anything, in exaggerated proportions in the winning hack. It is obvious, too, that the legs must be clean and strong, and in his movements he must be absolutely true and level.

It has been mentioned before that the show winning hack is usually a Thoroughbred; however it may be that, although it has prevailed for a number of years, this is something which will pass, giving way, perhaps, to the most refined type of Anglo-Arab or part-bred Arab.

Breed Society: The British Show Hack and Cob Association.

The modern Hackney is a harness-horse with a characteristic high-stepping, long, round striding trotting action, which is truly brilliant.

Its immediate ancestor is the Norfolk trotter. The Norfolk Roadster, as it came to be known, was an energetic, well-made animal bred for utility, used by farmers. It possessed speed and stamina, and had to be up to weight, often carrying not only the farmer to market but his wife as well, riding pillion behind him. The most famous of that breed was the 'Norfolk Cob', bred from Burgess's 'Fireaway' in the early 1820s. He is said to have trotted 38·6 km (24 miles) in the hour, and is definitely recorded as having done 3·2 km (2 miles) in 5 minutes 4 seconds. Another famous trotter 'Nonpareil', was driven 160 km (100 miles) in 9 hours 56 minutes 57 seconds.

As is obvious from its description, the Hackney has Arab blood in its veins, and almost every Hackney sire can trace its descent directly back to the Darley Arabian, through his son 'Flying Childers'. Another famous sire was 'Sampson', whose grandson, 'Messenger', was the foundation of the present American trotting horse. During the 19th century, with the advent of the railway, the Norfolk breed became extinct, but the Hackney itself became popular in other parts of England.

The ultimate origins of the Hackney, however, go back far into English history, the trotting horse, as distinguished from the ambler and the galloper, being recognized in very early times, for it was definitely mentioned as such in 1303. There was also at one time a strong infusion of Spanish Andalusian blood. The name itself is derived from the Norman French word *haquenée*.

Chief characteristics, in addition to brilliant and fiery paces, are: small, convex head, small muzzle; large eyes and small ears; longish, thick-set neck; powerful shoulders and low withers; compact body without great depth of chest; tail set and carried high; short legs and strong hocks well let down; well-shaped feet; fine silky coat. Most usual colours, dark brown, black, bay and chestnut. Height varies from 14·3 to 15·3 hands, sometimes reaching 16·2.

Both in motion and at rest it has highly distinctive and readily observable characteristics. Shoulder action is free, with a high, ground-covering knee action, the foreleg being thrown well forward, not just up and down, with that slight pause of the foot at each stride which gives it its peculiar grace of movement, appearing to fly over the ground. Action of the hind legs is the same to a lesser degree. In a good Hackney the action must be straight and true, with no dishing or throwing of the hoofs from side to side. At rest the Hackney stands firm and foursquare, forelegs straight, hind legs well back, so that it covers the maximum ground; the head is held high, ears pricked, with a general impression of alertness and of being on springs.

In these days of mechanized transport it would not be surprising if it had to be recorded that the Hackney Horse, which exists today purely as a pleasure horse, was declining to complete extinction at a rapid pace. Quite the reverse, however, can be recorded, the credit for which lies with the horse itself (and with the horse is included the Hackney Pony), with all its spectacular and dynamic action, and the large and increasing number of breeders and admirers of the Hackney. During the period between the wars, a steady improvement was noticed in the Hackney, and since the Second World War this has become even more pronounced.

This is a state of affairs which must give great satisfaction to all who follow the fortunes of the Hackney, which, by the way, is recognized as being, with the show jumper, the most popular entrant in the show ring, each in its own way providing a maximum of violent but controlled activity. It should be mentioned that this last general commentary upon this breed applies equally to the Hackney Pony, and although its evolution differs to some extent from that of the horse, it is a replica on a smaller scale.

Breed Society: The Hackney Horse Society.

The evolution of the Hackney Pony is somewhat obscure as to date, though it is in fact a smaller edition of the Hackney Horse, which is of some antiquity. It is generally believed that the pony's first appearance was through a 14-hand Hackney Pony stallion foaled in the North of England in 1866 and registered as 'Sir George'. It was sired by a horse of the purest Yorkshire blood named 'Sportsman', although nothing is known of the breeding of the dam. From such breeding, however, came perhaps the most spectacular exhibit to be seen in English horse shows today.

Owing to the decline of the use of the harness-horse and pony, which has been progressive in England for many years, the Hackney is seen almost exclusively in the show-ring, where it is most popular. There the demand is for the most extravagant action which it is possible to produce in a horse, and nothing short of this can carry the animal to any degree of success. The action must be spectacular, fluid and extravagant, with knees raised to the extremity and feet flung forward with rounded action, avoiding any heaviness of forehand or going into the ground. The hocks must be brought right under the body and raised almost to touch it. The whole effect must be arresting and startling, showing extreme brilliance. The best of these ponies fetch high prices both for the home and export trade.

The Hackney Pony must be of true pony type, especially as to the head, and the small horse, as distinct from the pony, must be avoided. Of late years, in spite of the development of more extravagant action, there is a tendency in the breed to lose a certain straightness of action, many otherwise good ponies going too close in front with hocks away.

Ponies whose action is not sufficiently extravagant for the show-ring find a not-too-ready market. To the extent that they can be absorbed into the harness market, they serve a very good purpose, for they are possessed of hard legs and will stand up to wear in spite of popular belief to the contrary. That they are active workers may be assumed. Owing to the enormous amount of muscular development in the hocks, the Hackney Pony was at one time much in demand as a show jumper, at which sport it excelled. Up to the early years of the present century the pony was much used by tradesmen for delivery purposes, owing to its flash appearance and the fact that it is an active and honest worker. In addition, it was looked upon as a good advertisement for any tradesman.

Description Pony character throughout. A long neck, good shoulders and a compact, strong body with hard limbs and well-defined tendons. Colours are mostly bays, browns and blacks.

Breed Society : The Hackney Horse Society.

The Hafflinger Pony is a Tyrolese breed and represents a small but very thick mountain horse, with plenty of bone and a neat head, which it usually carries close to the ground while climbing. Owing to its great qualities of strength, sure-footedness and quite good movement, it makes an excellent pack and draught horse, used to a great extent in the agriculture and forestry industries in the mountains.   Just before the Second World War it attracted a great amount of attention from the German authorities, who gave much support to its breeding.   The Hafflinger stallions were reared in the Central Stud at Piber (Austria).   The average height of the pony is just under 14 hands; it has a rather long body, and is usually palomino in colour.

The Hanoverian breed, as it is known today, is a
comparatively modern production, owing its origin
to the influence of our own Hanoverian kings, who,
from the time of George I down to 1837, took a
great interest in the horse of their native Hanover
and sent many English Thoroughbreds to cross
with the existing German breeds.

These breeds were sprung from the German
Great Horse of the Middle Ages, which was a
descendant of the animals that carried the Frankish
horsemen when, under Charles Martel, they met
and defeated the Saracens at the Battle of Poitiers
in 732, one of the decisive battles of the world.
The descent of these animals may be traced from
the Eastern and Southern European breeds of pre-
Christian times, mixed with the horses of a German

tribe, the Tencteri, who settled on the left bank of the Rhine about A.D. 100 and who 'were distinguished from all other German tribes by their love of horses and their finely organised cavalry.'

From the time of the Franks, the German horse developed and became the great war horse of European armoured chivalry, and the description given by the 16th-century writer Thomas Blundeville is worth recording:

The Almaine is commonlie a great horse, and though not finelie, yet verie stronglie made, and therefore more meete for the shocke than to pass a cariere, or to make a swift manage, because they are very grosse and heavie. . . . The desposition of this Horse (his heavy mould considered) is not evill, for he is verie tractable, and will labour indiffirentlie by the way, but his pace for the most part is a verie hard trot.

The horses of Flanders, Cleves and so on were all varieties of the same type.

With the advent of gunpowder and the disappearance of armour the type had to be modified again, and German breeders developed the 17th- and 18th-century light and heavy cavalry horse, falling into three main groups—Hanoverian, Mecklenburg and Danish.

This old Hanoverian breed was then, as we have seen, interbred with the English horses sent over by the Hanoverian Georges, and had finally disappeared by about the middle of the 18th century, to be replaced by the modern Hanoverian, whose pedigree contains Cleveland Bay and Thoroughbred blood.

There are few breeds of horses on the Continent better known than the Hanoverian.

The largest and strongest of the mountain and moorland group of breeds of Great Britain, the Highland pony is to be found in the highlands of Scotland and certain adjacent islands. The Highland is of great antiquity. It is said that after the Ice Age in Europe there was a movement of ponies towards the west from Northern Asia, the larger ones keeping to the north, now represented by the Scandinavian and Highland ponies, and the smaller going to the south, becoming known by the general term of Eastern Breeds.

Today the Highland pony may be divided into three types: the smaller ponies of Barra and the outer islands standing from 12·2 to 13·2 hands; the second class is the well-known riding-pony of some 13·2 to 14·2 hands; the largest and strongest are known as "Mainland" ponies, and stand about 14·2 hands. Highland ponies have had an infusion of alien blood, mostly Arabian.

As a worker the Highlander is immensely strong and very docile. It has always been used to carrying the deer for stalkers in the Highlands, and has been a great stand-by for the crofters in those parts. The pony is first-class for hill work on account of its sure-footedness, and is a well-balanced walker. It is pleasant to ride at its natural paces which are walking and trotting, but many tend to be on the 'forehand.'

Description Head, well carried, attractive and broad between prominent, bright eyes; short between eyes and muzzle, with wide nostrils. Ears short and well set. In profile the breadth, rather than the length, of the head and jawbone should be pronounced. Neck, strong and not short, crest arched, with flowing mane; throat clean, not too fleshy. Shoulders, well set back; withers not too pronounced. Body: back short, with slight natural curve; chest deep; ribs deep, well sprung, carried well back. Quarters and loins powerful, thighs short and strong. Tail, strong and well set on, carried gaily, with a plentiful covering of hair almost to the ground. Legs, flat in the bone, with a slight fringe of straight silken feather ending in a prominent tuft at the fetlock joint. Forelegs placed well under the weight of the body; forearm strong and knee broad. Oblique pasterns, not too short; and broad, firm, horny hoofs. Hocks, broad, clean, flat and closely set. Action free and straight. Colour, black, brown, chestnut colour with silver mane and tail; varying dun or grey with no white markings. The eel stripe along back is typical, but not always present.

Breed Society : The Highland Pony Society.

Another very good German breed, suitable for both riding and driving, is the Holstein Horse, whose origin is supposed to date back to the 13th century. The horse was bred on very good pastures of alluvial origin on the right bank of the River Elbe, which were very suitable for providing a powerful animal, and in the 16th to 18th centuries this breed was in high esteem not only at home but also abroad, particularly for export to France. The breed fetched good prices and was exported in large numbers, but afterwards it deteriorated.

According to E. Iverson's *Abstracts of Animal Breeding* (March 1939, p. 6), 'Das Holsteiner Pferd, 1937':

From 1825 onwards a reorientation of breeding took place, particularly owing to the introduction of the Yorkshire Coach Horse. The resulting compact conformation combined with a satisfactory gait proved successful, and an increased demand for Holstein horses again caused a serious dearth of breeding of uniform quality. This led to the organisation of breeders and of the central stud at Traventhal. Contrary to the usual policy in German "warm-blood" breeding, the English Thoroughbred influence in Holstein is negligible, but half-bred stallions contributed to the present excellence of the blood.

Usually of brown colouring, the Holstein horse is a very fine, strong animal, with good legs, free action, endurance and gait, and its conformation is different from that of other German 'warm-blood' horses. Although of slow growth it enjoys now a very good reputation as a light-draught horse and even show jumper. Just before the Second World War there was a great demand for the Holstein in South America and other countries, while in Germany it was mostly used as an artillery horse.

As with the Hanoverian, the Holstein was always a popular horse and one that was found in great numbers, but like all ride-and-drive horses the breed has suffered more seriously than the true riding-horse as the result of mechanization. As has been pointed out, it has a resemblance to the Hanoverian, and is seen at times as a very handsome horse, although others have not attained a very high standard of looks. The Traventhal Stud was closed in 1961.

As equine skulls dating from the period of the Magyar invasion show, the Hungarian horse had prevailing characteristics of the wild tarpan (*Equus caballus gmelini*) with certain admixture of the blood of the Mongolian horse (*Equus przevalskii*). It was a hardy, primitive breed, late maturing, small, and possessed of great endurance. Later on, numerous Turkish invasions were responsible for introducing to the Hungarian horse a strong dose of oriental blood by crossing with Arab, Turkish and Persian stallions. The Hungarian farmers' horse is a descendant of this horse, although some changes have occurred in it because of the large number of half-bred horses which spread their influence all over the country.

It is a light horse standing roughly about 15 hands, with very good strong legs, intelligent head and lively temperament, used for both saddle and harness. It is bred in a rather rough manner, fed only on maize, oat straw and grass, and taken in to work as a two-year-old. This native stock was excellent material for establishing the new, popular Hungarian breeds, which were bred on a large scale for military purposes in the days of the Austro-Hungarian Empire.

The best Hungarian breed, which can in fact be considered as a special kind of Arab half-bred, is the Shagya. The name is derived from a stallion of that name which was responsible for the foundation of the breed. There is a tradition still adhered to that stallions of this breed have the same name with the addition of a Roman number, which shows to which generation after the original Shagya the horse belongs. Genetically this breed was very well established, thanks to much careful inbreeding. The Shagya is an extremely hardy horse, standing from 14 to 15 hands, an excellent mover, thriving on very little food and having not only looks but also most of the qualities of Arab. In colour most of them are grey. The horse, being the best light-cavalry and light-carriage horse, is bred all over Hungary and in the neighbouring countries. The main stud is in Babolna, near Bana. Many of the Shagya stallions after 1918 were imported to Poland and caused great improvement to appear in Polish horse-breeding, especially in the southern part of Poland.

It is not necessary to point out perhaps that horses have been used for the chase for very many centuries, for they have always offered the obvious and the most convenient medium to man seeking and pursuing his quarry, whether boar, stag, fox or hare. The type of animal ridden is now—and always has been—dependent upon the animal hunted, the size and weight of the rider, and the nature of the country hunted. It is clear that the hunter, strictly speaking, is of no particular breed.

If, however, the hunter is considered for hunting at its best in England, Ireland, or the United States of America, then the Thoroughbred horse is the one which is considered essential for a country, especially where fences are big and hounds hunt in the main over grass, such as is typified by the shires of England. Apart from this, hunting countries which ride 'heavy', that is, where the going may be expected to be deep and holding, obviously require a short-legged and powerful animal; and to generalize still further, a hilly country requires not only a horse with exceptional shoulders, but one that has natural balance, if its rider is to hunt with safety as well as comfort. In a confined and trappy country where there is much woodland and the fences are very varied in character, a handy horse of reasonable height is indicated; and it should be emphasized that one of the most important requirements of a hunter in any of the countries suggested, or indeed in any country, good, bad or indifferent, is a horse with plenty of natural intelligence, for a day with hounds can hardly be enjoyed anywhere, at any time, without both horse and rider finding themselves in some sort of difficulty, where it is almost invariably the horse which must save the situation by instant application of its sense of self-preservation.

The show hunter of today, according to British standards, is grouped into three classes—light-weight, 82·5 kg (13 st) and under; middle-weight, over 82–5 kg and not exceeding 92 kg (14 st, 7 lb); and the heavy-weight hunter, over 92 kg. Perhaps the most admired—and certainly the most expensive—hunter, whether a show horse or not, is a Thoroughbred horse up to as much weight as possible, and the more weight he can carry the greater is his market value.

In judging a hunter, a few essentials of vital importance must always be borne in mind. It must, of course, be absolutely sound and stand on the best of legs; its body must be generous and sufficiently ample to allow heart, lungs and so on to perform their duties under conditions of great exertion; and, further, it should give its rider as long a rein as possible. Its head must be of the right size and its neck obviously of the correct length to assist with the many acts of balancing which it must perform during a hunt. Almost of more importance, if it is possible, the high-class hunter must be courageous and bold, tireless and, as it is said, always able to find an 'extra leg' if in trouble. It must not chance its fences, but must stand back and boldly attack each one as it meets it; such being the case, it is obvious that if the right temperament is there the ideal horse to hunt is the Thoroughbred, or as near as may be to one that is Thoroughbred.

The value of a hunter must in the main be dependent on its ability to perform in a way required of a good hunter following hounds. This, however, does not apply to the show hunter in England, for no certificate or evidence of any kind is required of its performance in that direction, nor is it required to jump obstacles in the show-ring, although now from time to time at some shows this may be a condition of entry.

In these circumstances, the judging must be based on conformation and, to some extent, type, and largely on action. Furthermore, the judge will ride the exhibit to discover how it would probably behave in the heat of the chase and whether it would be in good control at its fences. How well or ill it can actually perform is a matter for decision by the judge.

Breed Society: The Hunters' Improvement and National Light Horse Breeding Society.

The ponies of Iceland are not indigenous, but immigrants, and their history is almost exactly contemporaneous with that of the inhabitants. An early settler in Iceland was Ingolf, a Norwegian *jarl*, who moved there with his family in about 875. Others followed from Norway, and at the end of the 9th century, settlers went from Orkney, Shetland and the Western Isles.

These settlers brought with them their families, household goods and domestic livestock, including ponies. So there is good evidence that the horse was introduced into Iceland from both east and south-west—Norway and Ireland—and the present animal is a mixture of two early varieties of the Celtic type of horse which we find so widely distributed over north and west Europe. (See also Connemara, Norwegian, Shetland, Highland,

Scandinavian, etc.) The ultimate place of origin of the south-western or Hebridean stock was Ireland, for there was a good deal of traffic between Ireland and the Hebrides and Iceland. Horses figure also in the Icelandic sagas, two famous ones being Starkad's chestnut stallion and Gunnar's brown, described in the *Saga of Burnt Njal*.

The Norse settlers in Iceland, in addition to the ordinary domestic uses of their ponies, indulged in the pastime of horse-fighting. The same source tells that 'Starkad had a good horse of chestnut hue and it was thought that no horse was his match in fight'. And the development of the tragedy depends on the fight between that horse and Gunnar's brown and its sequel. They also ate horse-flesh on special occasions until their conversion to Christianity at the end of the 10th century.

Iceland ponies are usually graded into riding and pack and (to a less extent) draught, although the latter are all ridable if necessary. The riding ponies are broken to an ambling gait. They have been for the thousand or so years of their history the only means of transport in Iceland.

In appearance they are short and stocky, with large heads and intelligent eyes, very short, thick necks, and heavy mane and forelock, and are from 12 to 13 hands. They are hardy in the extreme and possess very keen sight. They also have a pronounced homing instinct, and the customary way of returning a pony after a long trek is to turn it loose, and it will usually find its way home within 24 hours. Little ordinary horse training or horse-mastership is possible with them, and the usual method of control is by voice. In character they are docile and friendly, although, like all these small pony breeds, they are sturdily independent by nature.

Attempts to produce a finer, more breedy type of Thoroughbred cross in order to produce a good child's pony have failed, the best characteristic of both strains being lost. It would seem that the Iceland pony is a mixture rather than a breed and will not breed true outside its own blood.

Mention should be made here of a similar type, the ponies of the Faroe Islands. Very much the same in appearance and character, their prevailing colours are dark brown and chestnut and occasionally black, while the most frequent colours of the Iceland pony are grey and dun.

Up to comparatively recent times there was a steady trade in England for the Iceland pony, many going to work in the pits, others finding themselves between the shafts working mostly in the towns. From the description given here of these small, sturdy ponies it will be correctly assumed that they gave very great satisfaction, and even today one hears the wish expressed that some Icelanders could be seen as in the old days. The student of the pony will note the close resemblance in outline, conformation and colour to many of the northern pony breeds—Scandinavian, Highland, Norwegian and, to a lesser extent, the Shetland and Connemara. In that group are gathered ponies which excel in a toughness rarely to be found elsewhere, certainly never to be exceeded.

Russia has a number of different breeds and
types of horses and ponies, at least fourteen, which
is not surprising considering its vast territory.
Nevertheless, we find at times one breed intermingling with another, or some which are produced by
tribal selection, such as the Iomud or Jomud.

Owing to its remoteness, and contrary to what
we find so frequently in almost every horse-breeding country throughout the world, the admixture
of Thoroughbred blood is little found in Russia.
Naturally it is only when we find a horse having
rather more quality that Thoroughbred or more
likely Arab blood is found, as in Strelets (*q.v.*).

The Iomud horses are descended from the same
ancient taproot as the Akhal-Teke breed, but have
been evolved by another Turkoman tribe, the
'Iomud'.   They differ from the Akhal-Teke (*q.v.*)
in being smaller, not so fast, and they are much
more fiery and highly strung.   They are run in
tabuns on the plains of Northern Turkmenia, and
have great powers of endurance, being able to withstand extremes of temperature ranging from fierce
summer heat to the rigours of the severest winters.
The Akhal-Teké have been used with success on
some Iomud horses which were not up to the high
standard desired, and this with excellent results,
and it is recorded that both breeds compete together in races and endurance tests.

Italy was never a horse-breeding country of any great note, although it was said that at one time many thousands of almost pure-bred Arabs and Barbs were kept by Pope Gregory the Great.   In the 16th and 17th centuries, in the district of Naples, there was established a Neapolitan breed which became quite famous, the great role in the foundation of this breed being played by Spanish horses.

King Henry VIII of England apparently imported some Neapolitan stallions, and was also sent some mares by Francisco Gonzaga, Marquis of Mantua, who bred horses at Mormolata on Lake Mincio.   The 16th-century writer Thomas Blundeville mentions the 'Neapolitan and the Sardinian', saying that in their gentle nature and docility, their comely shape, their courage, their sure-footmanship, their well reining, their lofty pace, their clean trotting, their strong galloping and their swift running, they excel numbers of other races, even so far as the fair greyhound the foul mastiff curs.

It is said that the Neapolitan horses were similar to the famous Spanish Ginetes but bigger, and with paces similar to their Moorish contemporaries in Northern Africa. The Neapolitans were said to take longer to mature than horses of other races, being best when put into training when six or seven years old, and they maintained their perfection considerably longer than other horses.

Since the middle of the 18th century horse-breeding in Italy was very much neglected, and was only revived to some extent between the World Wars. The Hafflinger is very popular today and is also used for the improvement of horses in the mountainous regions of Parma, Piacenza and Como. In Le Murge a large, robust Murgese horse, which is of oriental origin, is bred and much improved by careful selection. In Apulia local mares are bred to Salerno and Maremma stallions with an admixture of English Thoroughbred blood carefully added, thus resulting in strong saddle and draught horses having a good appearance and excellent conformation.

It should be noted that the island of Sardinia produces a pony of considerable worth, which in appearance is very similar to the Corsican ponies. They are bred in a semi-wild state and are very hardy. They stand approximately 13 to 14 hands, are bay in colour, and when exported usually fetch good prices. They are used both for harness work and riding. Heavy cart-horses are seen mostly in the Po Valley and are usually not bred in Italy, as all heavy work in that country is carried on by oxen and mules. Other very good horses are the Sicilians, which are of Arab type with Spanish and Italian influence.

It should be mentioned that just previous to the Second World War Italy achieved great success in breeding racehorses, an outstanding example being the very well-known and successful 'Nearco', sire of 'Dante', and another well-known and fashionable stallion, 'Donatello II'.

Since Italy lies so much to the southernmost part of Europe, it is surprising to find that the strong, 'cold-blooded' draught horse exists and thrives there, for the tendency is for the lighter or 'hot-blooded' types to predominate in such regions.

It is well known that Italy has produced horsemen of outstanding reputations, not only as instructors in equitation, but also in show jumping, and their horse shows are among the best organized in the world. It seems, however—and indeed this applies to some other nations as well—that they must rely to some extent on the imported horses for their requirements. In this connection it should be noted that the show jumper is not a breed, and that all horses, whether pure-bred or cross-bred, are potential show jumpers.

As its name suggests, the horse originated in Jutland, where it is still the breed most commonly used. From there it was taken to the Danish Islands at a very early date. Skilful and consistent selection has improved it to a very high level. The founder sire was 'Oppenheim LXII', imported from England; he became the ancestor of some of the best stallion lines, within which were 'Aldrup Munkedal', 'Hövding', 'Prins of Jütland', 'Fjandbo', 'Skjalden', 'Lune Dux', 'Hof', and 'Himmerland Eg'.

The Jutland, which has an excellent temperament, and is of medium size, is primarily an agricultural horse, although it has also been used for town work. The body is of good width; legs are massive, with soft, smooth hair. Its colour is predominantly chestnut; at one time other colours were to be seen.

Kabarda or Kabardin The Kabarda is one of the most sure-footed of all mountain riding horses and is found in the mountain regions of the northern Caucasus. When crossed with the Thoroughbred it is known as the Anglo-Karbardin and is then used to improve other breeds. The colour is generally bay. The Karbarda possesses a first-class sense of direction, is courageous and sagacious, and has a marked independence of character.

Karabair and Lokai The Karabair is bred in Usbekistan. It is an old native breed. There is the riding type and the heavier strong harness horse which can also be used under the saddle. The Lokai is native to Tadshikstan and although used as a riding horse, the chief uses are for pack transport.

This beautiful breed is found in the Caucasian
districts, and has greatly contributed in the past to
the improvement of the Don horses (*q.v.*).   They
are similar to the highest class of Persian horse,
that is to say they are predominantly Arabian
in conformation, and with the dished face of the
Arab as opposed to the straight profile of the
Persian.   Their characteristic golden colour is also
to be found in another Russian breed, the Akhal-
Teké (*q.v.*).   This most admired colour, together
with admirable conformation, makes the Karabakh
breed one of the most beautiful in the world.

Ancient fossil remains of horses have been found in the Siwalik foothills of the Himalayas. Today, the Kathiawari and Marwari strains of horses are found all over India, but mostly in the hard, dry, northern plains from the Indus to the Ganges and south to the Deccan. They are generally wretched little creatures, thin, weedy, very narrow, the front legs 'coming out of the same hole', as the saying goes, seldom more than 13 to $13\frac{1}{2}$ hands high, but with feet and legs of cast iron, amazing toughness and powers of endurance and the ability to live on next to nothing. India is not ranked amongst the great horse-breeding countries and horsemanship is not a national characteristic.

The Kathiawari and the Marwari, being very similar in ancestry and characteristics, can be taken together.   Mention should first be made, however, of the Unmol (meaning 'priceless'), varieties of which were bred in the northern Punjab.   They are traditionally supposed to be descended from horses brought by Alexander the Great when he invaded India, and are described as being very strong, elegant and shapely, with a long mane and compact body. The pure breed, however, is now practically extinct, those few that survive being well mixed with imported Thoroughbred and Arab blood.   The Kathiawari takes its name from the peninsula of Kathiawar on the north-west coast of India between the Gulfs of Cutch and Cambay. The common ancestors of the Kathiawari and the Marwari (which is found in Rajputana) are said to be a shipload of Arab horses which was wrecked on the west coast of India.   These horses ran wild in the jungles and plains of Kathiawar and Marwar, and naturally mixed with the indigenous 'country-bred' pony.   The Arab strain certainly shows itself in the best of both these breeds, which have also special characteristics of their own, the inward pointing of the tips of the ears, which almost meet, and the prevalence of sickle hocks.   They run from 14 to 15 hands, and the most usual colours are chestnut, brown, bay, grey, piebald and skew-bald, with some creams.   The best bred of the Kathiawaris are in demand for racing, and in the days of height limits were used for polo.   It is not improbable that one of the colleagues of Kipling's 'Maltese Cat' was a Kathiawari.

The Marwari figures prominently as a war horse in the annals of Rajasthan, and in the Middle Ages horse-breeding was the chief occupation in Marwar.

The 16th-century writer Abul Fazar, in his *Ain-i-Akbari*, mentions that the entire Rajput population of this region formed an imperial service cavalry of over 50,000 horses.

Like all 'country-breds' they are tough and hardy, possessing considerable staying powers and having an easy gait, and, be it said, an uncertain temper.

As neither of these two breeds had been used extensively by the British for polo or any other purpose for a number of years previously, it cannot be said that the withdrawal of the British Army can have had any particular effect on the numbers of ponies bred. Having regard to the wild nature of the country which is their habitat and the primitive agricultural needs of the people, it may well be that these ponies will hold their own as well as any in these present times, when the horse and pony population of the world is ever decreasing.

If this proves to be the case, it may happen that some grading-up by the introduction of 'foreign' blood may take place, as it has in the past.

In the Baltic states of Estland and Livland, now dominated by the U.S.S.R., there were ponies standing about 13 to 13·2 hands high, which were native to these states.   The mares were crossed with Arab and Ardennais stallions and the result was the so-called Klepper, a somewhat larger and strong cobby horse of considerable stamina.

In considering this type it is as well to bear in mind that by the admixture of alien blood from time to time, and influenced also by soil and climate, several variations of the type have been evolved, each bearing its own name.   Nevertheless, all have retained a certain similarity and each one is stamped with the characteristics of the original wild horse.   In consequence the ability of the Klepper, or of any of its associate breeds, to exist on the most meagre rations, their hardiness and their abnormal strength for size are very pronounced.   Their prepotency in stamping their type on their progeny is perhaps second only to that of the Arab, and, despite their normally grim and rigorous existence, they are noted for having exceptionally long lives.

The characteristic colour of many North European breeds is dun, with the eel-stripe through the back to the tail, and the mane and tail black.   With these breeds is included the Klepper, and there is little doubt that the type can to some extent be classed as one of the great family, with many so different in type, that runs through all the northern regions.

These Kleppers contributed to the breeding of the Viatka pony (*q.v.*), 13 to 14 hands, and of two types—Obvinka and Kazanka; all are of good conformation and looks, strong, hardy and fast.

This breed is an old Danish one, exclusively
confined to spotted horses, and it seems that the
peculiar form of these spots, described by the
British Spotted Horse Society as 'leopard', 'snow-
flake' and 'blanket', are to be found in the Knabstrup.

During the Napoleonic wars, Spanish troops
were stationed in Denmark for a short period, and
one of their officers left behind a spotted mare,
which, although relegated to the honest work required by a butcher in the delivery of meat, proved
outstanding both as to speed and endurance. A
Major Villars Lunn, the owner of an estate known
as Knabstrup, subsequently bought this chestnut
mare, which had 'blanket' markings with a white

mane and tail and was of English hunter rather than
of Spanish type.   This officer and his father before him were great breeders of horses of riding
type, always laying special stress on hardiness,
speed and endurance, their stock originating from
that of the famous old Royal Frederiksborg Stud
which was of Spanish-Arab-Barb type similar to the
Lipizzaner.

So it was that the butcher's mare, which was
named 'Flaebehoppen', became the foundation
mare of the spotted Knabstrup breed.   In 1812
she was put to a Frederiksborg stallion of Palomino colour and produced a colt 'Flaebehingsten',
which became the foundation stallion of the breed,
and he, too, had similar colouring and the markings of the original mare.   It is said that this horse,
while having similar colourings which were of
lighter shades, had a general and rather peculiar
metallic appearance and was described as having
'more than twenty colours'.

In Denmark, interest in this breed is very considerable, more than one Society having been
formed, and there are a number of stud farms in
the country.

The picture shown is of a stallion, "Silverking
II," being "leopard" with black spots.   Needless
to say, with the inevitable variations which occur
in all spotted markings, the Knabstrup is sought as
a circus horse and may be seen performing in Great
Britain.   A direct descendant of 'Silverking', a
chestnut blanket filly with white mane and tail, was
shipped to England in the 1950s.

The average height of the Knabstrup is 15·3
hands.

There are several native breeds of ponies in Poland which go under the general name of *konik*, which means 'Small horse'. These breeds have their own names: Huçul, Zmudzin, and the older strain called the *Panje* horse. The Konik cannot properly be described as a particular breed but no doubt it is descended from the wild Tarpan (*q.v.*).

Apart from the Konik, the greater proportion of the Polish peasant horses belong to the type of *Mierzyn*, which means a medium horse between two sizes, usually 13 to 14 hands. The small size, as in all these native pony breeds, is more than compensated by their outstanding qualities of hardiness, endurance, ability to live on next to nothing, vitality and great fertility, which they always transmit unimpaired to their progeny. Both the Konik and the Mierzyn are remarkably long-lived, and capable of work up to a considerable age.

The Latvian breed has been developed in the Baltic state of Latvia, U.S.S.R., by crossing the native draught horse with approved stallions of lighter breeds. This has resulted in a horse with substance and bone, good temperament and with an aptitude for jumping. It is claimed to be an ideal heavy-weight hunter. Having been bred mostly by small farmers, the majority of these horses are driven in harness. Their stamina and powers of endurance generally are outstanding. In considering the Latvian breed, as with the horses of Esthonia and Lithuania, reference is usually made to the North European breeds.

Bred and raised at Cantal, Corrèze, Pery-de-Dôme, Haute-Loire, Vienne, Haute-Vienne, Creuse and Indre, the Limousin Half-bred, though lacking the quality, has a great deal of the Anglo-Arab. It is the product of Limousin mares already up-graded and qualified as half-breds and English Thoroughbred, pure-bred Arab, Anglo-Arab or Anglo-Arab Half-bred studs. (A horse is qualified as a half-bred if it has a minimum 25 per cent of Thoroughbred or Arab blood.) After more than half a century of this, the breed is sufficiently fixed to perpetuate its traits without further cross-breeding.

The oriental origins of the horses of Limousin date back to the Moorish invasion of the 8th century. Under Napoleon I they were deservedly reputed to be excellent saddle horses; but under the Restoration the breed went into decline, until renewed alternate crossing with English Thoroughbred and Arab finally gave it uniformity.

Today's Limousin Half-breds, of varying degrees of English Thoroughbred and Arab blood, have a decidedly oriental character. Certain groups have an Anglo-Norman admixture, thereby gaining in size what they lose in quality. On the whole it is a good riding and light draught horse. Possessing all the general lines of the pure-bred Anglo-Arab and Anglo-Arab Half-bred, it is taller (average 16 hands) and of more generous build. Greys are becoming increasingly rare, with chestnut and bay predominating. This breed, like the other half-breds raised in France, is nowadays known in that country under the name of *Cheval de Selle Français*.

This famous breed is of Austrian origin, and takes its name from the place, Lipizza, where the stud farm of the same name was founded in 1580 by the Archduke Charles, son of the Emperor Ferdinand I.

The origin of this breed goes back to 1564, when there had been introduced into Austria a highly specialized type of horse, the Kladruber (taking its name from the stud farm of Kladrub in Bohemia), which was the result of a mixture of Spanish and Neapolitan blood. The characteristics of this breed were a heavy, big-boned frame, small head, round nose, curved or arched neck, and often drooping ears. The height was from 16 to 17 hands. The horses were bred for court use, to draw the royal carriages and to be ridden in processions and on state occasions. Owing to inbreeding they developed a number of defects, becoming very short-lived, liable to have poor feet and legs not strong enough for their size and weight. In spite of this, however, they continued in use until the break-up of the Austrian Empire in 1918, when they were all sold and the stud dispersed.

The Lipizzaner is derived from a cross between the Kladruber and a small Italian horse of Northern Italy—especially around Trieste and in Gorizia—with a later admixture of Arab blood. There are six famous lines: 'Pluto', 'Conversano', 'Neapolitan', 'Favory', 'Maestro' and 'Siglavy'. These are the animals which were used in the Spanish Riding School at Vienna, which was built for the Emperor Charles VI in 1735 by the architect Fischer von Erlach. It may be noted that the celebrated airs and exercises taught and practised there are not of Spanish origin, in spite of the name of the school, but were initiated by two great horsemen of the past, one English, William Cavendish, 1st Duke of Newcastle, author of *A New Method and Extraordinary Invention to Dress Horses* (1667), and the other French, Antoine de Pluvinel de la Baume, riding-master to Louis XIII and author of books on the art of riding.

The Lipizzaner is a very beautiful horse, nearly always grey. It is extremely shapely and elegant in appearance, with a longish body, well ribbed-up, strong quarters, rather heavy shoulders and neck, small head, good legs with plenty of bone. The nostrils are rather narrow, the eyes large and horizontal. The general impression is one of strength, grace and dignity. They are intelligent and very docile in disposition. By contrast with their ancestor, the Kladruber, Lipizzaners are long-lived, and their intensive training in high school work does not really begin until they are from five to seven years old.

Up to the Second World War the chief breeding-place of this breed was at the Hungarian State Stud at Babolna, near Bana, which was founded in 1789, when Hungary was part of the Austrian Empire. Breeding was carried on there, on a large scale, of Arabs and half-bred Arabs as well as of Lipizzaners. The general system was to breed from selected fillies on their reaching four years. After the first foaling the fillies were broken-in for driving, and those with the best performance continued as brood mares. Apart from its high school use the Lipizzaner is a magnificent carriage-horse and a good hunter and hack.

Since it has so much presence, especially under saddle, with its spectacular action and arresting colouring, not to mention its understanding nature and tractability, it is somewhat surprising that the Lipizzaner has not been used as a riding-horse in England.

So great is the reputation of the Lipizzaner and so world-wide the knowledge of its association with the Spanish Riding School at Vienna, that little more need be said. Long after many types or breeds of note have ceased to exist, the probability is that the Lipizzaner will be found displaying the traditional airs of the Spanish Riding School as it has done for over three centuries.

The Manipur Pony takes its name from the state of that name in Assam where it has been bred from time immemorial. Doubts to the contrary notwithstanding, its claim to be a distinct breed is supported by historical evidence as well as by its appearance. Early manuscripts record that the breed existed at least as far back as the 7th century, when the reigning king of Manipur introduced the game of polo, played on ponies bred in his state.

Major-General Sir James Johnstone, in *My Experience in Manipur and the Naga Hills* (1896), wrote:

Manipur in olden days possessed a famous breed of ponies, larger and better bred than the so-called Burmese ponies that came from the Shan States. On these ponies were mounted the formidable cavalry that in the last century made Manipur feared throughout Upper Burma and enabled her rulers on more than one occasion to carry their victorious arms within sight of Ava, where their Raja Pamheita erected a stone pillar to commemorate the event.

It is quite probable that descendants of these same ponies accompanied yet another victorious army, the illustrious 14th, into Burma in 1945; for they were used, and valued, as military transport ponies in that most difficult of all battlegrounds.

From the general appearance of the Manipur it is reasonable to trace its descent from the Mongolian pony on the one hand, and from Arab blood on the other. And it is probable, too, that they do have some affinity, on that account, with the Shan ponies of Upper Burma. 'These two ponies', wrote Captain M. H. Hayes, 'appear to belong to a distinct breed, which seems to have no relationship with ponies of any other country except possibly those of Sumatra and Java'.

The following description, taken from *Indian Farming* (August 1942), remains accurate:

Though small in size, the animal possesses a proportionate body and is sturdy and sure-footed. The head is smart and carried well-up on a clean, strong, muscular neck. The face is fairly long and exhibits an alert, gentle appearance. The muzzle is fairly broad with well-dilated nostrils. The chest is broad and the ribs amply sprung. The legs are proportionate in size and of fine quality. Knees and hocks are strong, the shanks clean and straight, and the pasterns possess a gradual and proportionate slope. The animal measures 11 to 13 hands in height and the body-weight is about 650 lb (295 kg).

The prime object of German horse-breeding was to produce the type of horse which could serve first for military purposes and in peace-time could be useful as a working animal. Thus, besides a few breeds of 'cold-blood' horses like the now nearly extinct Rhenish or one-time Mecklenburg, which during wars served as heavy artillery horses, many 'warm-blood' breeds were selectively bred, such as East Prussian, Hanoverian, Holstein and others, which would answer all military requirements. They represent the cavalry or light-draught type of horse, standing from 15·2 to 16·3 hands, with good bone, being good weight carriers with easy action.

Today, the Mecklenburg horse is a 'warm-blood' horse got by 'warm-blood' stallions out of 'warm-blood' mares and bred by breeders organized as 'The Association of Mecklenburg Warm-blood Breeders'. The Mecklenburg horse passed through several stages. Once a heavy type of horse, in the middle of the 19th century it represented a good saddle-horse which was, unfortunately, very much deteriorated by the introduction and bad management of the English Thoroughbred. With its excellent pastures, Mecklenburg was used not only as the breeding country for 'warm-blood' horses, but also as a rearing ground for the 3,000 or so Hanoverian foals which were taken there each year.

Reviewing the postion as described, it will be seen that the Mecklenburg, like so many of the German breeds, has passed through many stages as the result of endeavours made to improve the breed by upgrading, coupled with the desire to produce a certain standard or type. Like so many of the country's equine products, the Mecklenburg shows admirable substance and bone. Since in the past the object has been to breed a general-purposes horse, with a strong emphasis on one suitable for cavalry or artillery, it is a matter for conjecture what type will now be evolved in East Germany, in view of the almost complete mechanization of the Army. It may be that with such excellent pasturage the country may concentrate on producing a riding-horse which, as has been shown, would not be foreign to the Mecklenburg breed.

This horse, or rather pony, among the most ancient of the types of *Equus caballus*, is to be found, both domesticated and feral, all over Mongolia, that vast, desolate area reaching from Manchuria in the east to Turkestan in the west, bounded by Siberia on the north and by Tibet and China to the south.   These ponies are exceedingly plentiful, being kept and bred in huge numbers by the Buriats and other Mongolian tribes, and, as may be expected in this inhospitable region, are extremely hardy and enduring.

In the eastern parts of Mongolia they are much in demand for export to China for racing and polo. There they are also crossed with other imported foreign breeds, from which has been produced the so-called China pony (illustrated here) which is not really a breed at all. In the west, Mongolian ponies have undoubtedly mingled in the past with Arabs to produce the Turkoman horses of Turkestan. To the south in Tibet and in the Himalayas their influence is also seen in the hill ponies of those regions, Spiti, Bhutan, Yarkand, and so on, which are all certainly closely related to the Mongolian. Nor does its influence end there. The animals of Burma and Malaysia are not indigenous to those countries, and there is no doubt that they derive in part from Mongolian stock. Even the famous Manipur breed has its ultimate origin from it.

The nomad owners of these ponies, while they breed them in large numbers, do not take any special pains to improve the stock, and certainly do not waste any time or money on feeding. The pony has to live on whatever it can pick up, which is not much and is tough at that. Consequently the teeth are usually very much worn down. Stallions are always animals selected by the breeders, but no attention is paid to the mares.

The average height of the Mongolian stallion is about 13·1 hands, but varies between 12·2 and 13·3 hands. The lowest heights seem to be found usually to the east along the China border, and the best in the northern districts.

In appearance they have heavy heads and shoulders and smallish eyes, thick necks, deep chests, well-sprung ribs, good quarters and loins and legs, with plenty of bone. Their hoofs are iron hard, though they are apt to be abnormally worn down by the hard and stony going. Mane and crest are coarse, coats long and shaggy, with flowing forelocks and tails that sweep the ground. The tails are thick-haired at the roots.

The ancestry of this American breed of light horse has caused a great amount of controversy over many years, but a measure of agreement has now been reached and it seems that the horse 'Justin Morgan' (originally named 'Figure'), owned by Thomas Justin Morgan, was foaled in 1789 in the Green Mountain country of Vermont, U.S.A. This bay, standing 14·2 hands, reproduced to type, character and conformation with extreme exactness, and won great fame and popularity, resulting in the service of large numbers of mares. The horse died in 1821, having established one of America's most famous general purpose breeds. The defined height is 14 to 15 hands.

Breed Society: Morgan Horse Club.

The term 'Mustang' was applied primarily to the feral or semi-feral horses of the plains of western America, but has been extended to include the herds on the pampas of South America as well. The derivation of the word is from the Spanish *mestengo*, meaning 'stranger', which in turn comes from the Spanish *mesta*, the name given to associations of graziers, one of whose functions was the appropriation of wild cattle which had attached themselves to the tame herds.

Like the word, the horse in historic times in America is of Spanish origin, and the animals which Cortés brought over from Cuba in 1519 were the first true horses ever to be seen in the New World. When the 'caballeros' of Cortés charged them, the Aztecs thought the gods had come down to earth, and fled in terror; and it is no exaggeration to say that without the horse Cortés could not have conquered Mexico or Pizarro, later, Peru. Other horses were introduced later by the Spaniards into Florida, by Ponce de Leon and by De Soto, Coronado and others, into the unknown hinterland of North America west of the Mississippi, becoming in due course Texas, Arizona, Colorado, etc. There is a complete list of the horses of Cortés which indicates that these, and by inference the later importations, were of Spanish blood, going back to Saracen (Arabian and Barb) ancestry.

During the adventures and misadventures of the *conquistadores*, many of their horses strayed or were captured by the Indians, and it is from them there grew, multiplying in a surprising manner in the three centuries up to 1819 (less than a hundred generations), the vast herds of feral and half-tamed horses which roamed the great plains at the beginning of the American pioneering times, and which made the American Indian the superb natural horseman that he was and is. To all these animals the comprehensive name of Mustang is given. There were various types within this term, the best being that known as the Indian Pony, a product of Indian breeding and selection. The term 'Bronco' (from the Spanish word meaning rough and rude), originally applied to the wildest and most untamable Mustangs—hence the phrase 'Bronco-busting'—has now come to apply to all these types equally with Mustangs.

The original Mustang was a small horse, seldom more than 14·2 hands in height and from 272 to 363 kg (600 to 800 lb) in weight. In common with all these small utility breeds, whether in the East or in the West, they were nothing much to look at, scraggy and rough, of uncertain temper, but hardy and courageous, and apparently built of cast iron. Occasional throwbacks to their original remote Arabian ancestry were known to appear, becoming legendary figures for their outstanding size, beauty and speed. Every known colour was represented and many strange shades and combinations, of which again only the East has the like to show. Once broken and domesticated, the Mustang was a useful light saddle-horse, and was the original cow pony.

Today the true Mustang has been largely succeeded by the modern range horse, the result of the crossing of a diversity of strains—Thoroughbred, Arab, Standard, Morgan, Quarter and others. Though this may be true as a general statement, the plain-looking and rough and workmanlike horse of the true Mustang type *does* still exist, remaining the useful, if at times very wild, servant it always was, and it is good to know that the old-time romance of the Wild West is thus not completely lost. By no manner of means is the cowboy of today mounted on beautiful Palominos, or flashily-marked Pintos, as American films would often have us believe. It is worth noting here in connection with cow-ponies that the Arab on account of the soundness of its legs, is increasingly used for cutting-out cows on the ranch.

The Mustang has figured much in the annals of the plains, and certainly in fiction and film. Because of this a certain romance has been built around the breed, and it is to be hoped that its existence will justify the breed's continuance.

Of Britain's nine mountain and moorland breeds, the New Forest Pony is, apart from the Highland, the largest. Its ancestry is uncertain and largely conjectural. Wild horses were mentioned as living in the Forest in Canute's reign, and there can be no doubt that they have been there continuously ever since.

Today the New Forest Pony roams at will over some 24,280 ha of 'forest' in Hampshire, though in fact the land is mostly bare of trees and offers the poorest pasture to the ponies, consisting in the main of heather and poor or rank grass. This has much effect on them, causing them to be hardy and economical feeders when brought off the Forest to 'family' life. The breed has been subject to a considerable amount of 'improving' by various breeds, and Queen Victoria in 1852 lent an Arab stallion, 'Zorah', which was in the Forest for eight years. But no alien stallions have been turned out there for over 50 years and the pony has become of a definite type and increasingly, it would appear, breeds true to it. 'Marske', the sire of 'Eclipse', was kept by a farmer in the New Forest district from 1765 to 1768, until 'Eclipse' became famous.

The New Forest ponies, as with other native breeds, play a most important part as foundation stock. Bred to survive the constant struggle for existence, they develop acute intelligence, courage and resource. They are used to picking their way over rough ground and are consequently very sure-footed. Accustomed to seeing many tourists in the New Forest, they are less shy of mankind than other mountain and moorland breeds; they have also become immune to every kind of road terror and thus make the safest possible mounts for children when properly broken-in.

Description The New Forest can be any colour except piebald or skewbald, and is a good riding type of pony. The head is well set on and the neck a little short from throat to chest, but the good, laid-back shoulder gives plenty of length of rein. The back is short and the loins and quarters strong; tail is well set on, though not exaggeratedly high; the forearm and second thigh good, short cannon bones and good feet. The pony should have plenty of bone and straight but not exaggerated action. There are two sizes:

Type A: Ponies up to 13·2 hands; ideal as children's hunting ponies; with quality.

Type B: 13·2 hands to 14·2 hands, with plenty of bone and substance; a strong type of pony able to carry adults.

Breed Society: The New Forest Pony Breeding and Cattle Society.

This attractive pony is one of the most distinctive and interesting breeds found throughout Europe. Actually two types of this breed are recognized, the *fjord-hest* of western Norway and the *doele-hest* or "valley horse" of the interior. Both have the same characteristics, but the ancient original type seems to be the one of the west.

The chief feature of the breed is, of course, the distinctive colour, between cream and dun. A dark dorsal stripe runs from tail to forelock through the mane, which is usually clipped to 4–5 inches to stand up in a fine crest. The legs are dark, and occasionally zebra markings occur. Bays and browns are also found, but dun is the prevailing and ancestral colour. Height about 14 hands.

The Fjord pony has a well-shaped head with a broad and flat forehead, big eyes and eyebrows and a sharp cheek ridge. The head is rather large but seldom rough. The Fjord pony has small truncated ears that are rather broadly placed. The neck is short and rough. Consequently the connection between head and neck is rather stiff. The neck is well-raised. The withers are rather short and round. The back is of medium length with well-developed muscles. Long backs with less well-developed muscles are unpopular in breeding. The croup is rather narrow and rounded. The outer corner of the hip is rather far forward as compared with the inner corner. This makes the croup somewhat narrow, but it also, on the other hand, makes the pony more strongly coupled. The thighs are muscular but often rather shallow. Long second thighs and bent hocks are to be avoided in breeding. The legs are dry and clean and a little coarse. The movement is light with a rapid change of feet. Most Fjord ponies are thrifty and easily fed and they are therefore well suited for smaller farms and for vegetable gardens both in Norway and in other countries.

By nature the Norwegian pony is docile and friendly and fond of company. Its pace is akin to a shuffling trot and it has a will of its own, but it is hardworking and tireless. It is used mostly for draught, either in quaint, low carts with four very small wheels or, for passengers, in a species of two-wheeled dogcart or the *Cajol*, which takes two people one behind the other—nevertheless it can be quite a good ride.

The ponies are never clipped and never rugged. In the winter they are housed in communal stables with cattle, pigs and other livestock, and are fed on hay only, unless timber hauling or other specially heavy work is to be done, when they are given oats and bran.

This is one of the heaviest of the German 'warm-blood' breeds and is bred on the same lines as the East Fresian.   Both trace their ancestry to the Friesian of Holland and so through this breed to Spanish and Oriental stallions.   Oldenburg horses are big with good action covering much ground. They were used as artillery horses during the First World War and subsequently in agriculture. Today the Oldenburg horse has become somewhat lighter since the Thoroughbred stallion 'Lupus', winner of the German Derby, was successfully used.   These horses are bred throughout West and East Germany, Denmark, Holland and Austria.

The originator of this famous breed of Russian trotters was Count Alexius Grigorievich Orlov, a Russian nobleman who was born in 1737 and died in 1808. He was renowned for his great strength and dexterity, and was a man of many interests besides the horse. He was concerned with his brother Gregory in the conspiracy of 1762 which led to the deposition and death of Czar Peter III, and was said to have been his actual murderer. He also commanded the Russian fleet which annihilated the Turks at Chesme in 1770. When he died he left 30,000 serfs and an estate worth five million roubles.

After his more violent activities he appears to have turned his attention to horse-breeding, and in 1777 evolved the breed which for ever after was to be known by his name when his other exploits were forgotten. He produced the Orlov Horse by crossing the following bloods: English Thoroughbred, Arab, Dutch, Danish and Mecklenburg. The first stallion was an Arab, called 'Smetanka', which was put to a Dutch mare from whom was bred a stallion called 'Polkan'. The first Trotter out of the latter's progeny was a stallion out of a black Dutch mare which was named 'Bars First'. This horse is considered to be the head of the Orlov breed. There were further admixtures of Dutch, English and Arab blood.

Trotting has always been a popular sport in Russia, and in pre-Revolution Russia the Orlov breed was developed for that purpose. As it is known now, the breed has two definite lines, a heavy type, which is predominantly black, and a slighter type, with more pronounced Arab features, which is usually grey. The latter has been more successful on the race-track and leads in speed records. So far as is known at present, the fastest mile (1·6 km) in Russia has been trotted in 2 minutes 6 seconds, which is still a good way behind the American record of 1 minute 55 seconds. (See Standard Bred.)

A good Orlov is very handsome, with a small head, very Arabian in appearance, broad chest, longish back, good well-rounded quarters and strong muscular legs. The height goes up to 17 hands.

At the beginning of the century the type was becoming a little degenerate, longer in the body and legs, and with decreasing stamina. New colours, dark brown and dark chestnut, also made their appearance. During the Revolution the proletarian zeal of the Bolsheviks extended to

thoroughbred horses as well as to human aristo-
crats, and many were destroyed.   Common sense
and sporting instinct, however, seem to have prevailed in time, and the breed was saved and is still
carried on together with the sport of trotting racing.   Count Orlov's stud had been acquired by the
Czarist State, and under the name of the Khre-
novsky Stud was the central breeding place of the
Orlov Horse.   Before the Revolution there were
about 3,000 stud farms in Russia devoted to the
breeding of these Orlov Trotters.

This breed is another instance of the Arabian
Horse foundation, and it is characteristic of that
blood and a mark of its prepotency that the Orlov
head still bears the Arab stamp.

The Orlov achieved its greatest fame as a trotter,
and in the latter half of the last century was looked
upon as the supreme horse for that work.   But it
could not now compete on equal terms with the
strong commercial development of the trotting
horse for the race-track, mostly in America.   This
is a case of scientific development producing excessive speed to the exclusion of all else, and has
its counterpart in the Thoroughbred ousting the
Arab from the racecourse and polo ground, to the
loss, as many believe, of soundness and stamina.

Reference has been made to the 3,000 stud farms
in Russia devoted to the breeding of this horse—
an almost unbelievable number, by the way—but
it is quite impossible to say how many of these
still exist today.   The least that can be hoped is
that this world-famous breed still flourishes.

The term 'Palomino' as applied to this beautiful horse of North America, appropriately known
as 'the golden horse of the West', is not yet
strictly a breed, but a colour. This colour is
literally gold, though variations from a soft cream
or light blonde chestnut to the darker shades are
admissible.   There are five official shades of a
golden colour with a metallic sheen.   The mane
and tail should be very light, almost white, and
except for white on the face and legs no other
colours or markings are admitted; albino and pinto
parentage are forbidden.   The eyes are dark, and
blue or chalk eyes are not accepted.

The ultimate origin of this attractive colouring
goes back to remote ages, its being mentioned in
Homeric times.   For practical purposes, however,

it appears to be of Spanish origin from Saracen and Moorish stock, and there is no doubt that the type contains Arab and Barb blood. Horses of this colour became highly prized in Spain, and Queen Isabella, the sponsor of Columbus, encouraged their breeding. It is possible that such animals were taken to the West Indies by Columbus, but it is on record that Cortés had them in Mexico in 1519. In Spain these horses were called 'Ysabellas' in honour of the famous queen. It is said that they take their present name from one Juan de Palomino, to whom Cortés presented one of them.

They were rediscovered about a hundred years ago when the United States took possession of California in 1848 after the Mexican war. Then Palominos were used extensively as saddle-horses and for parade and spectacular purposes, and also for racing until ousted by the speedier Thoroughbred. Their vogue then declined until recent times, when they were rediscovered and taken up for their appearance and excellent riding qualities.

Apart from the colour the following are the main physical characteristics of the Palomino. General appearance is of Arab or Barb type, only larger and more solid. The height is from 15·2 to 16 hands, and weight from 544 to 725 kg (1,200 to 1,600 lb). Only horses of over 14·2 hands are admitted into the register. For the rest they have the normal points of a good horse, with a fine showy action under saddle, a mild, amenable disposition and good movement.

The breeding is generally a cross between Palomino and light chestnuts of the light horse breeds, and also Palomino to Palomino. A cross between a chestnut mare with light mane and tail and a

Palomino stallion will usually produce a Palomino foal in 80 per cent of such crosses. But the breeding is still in the experimental stage and by no means fixed. Foals are usually true Palomino at birth, with blue eyes. The colour changes somewhat with age, and the eyes darken. Manes and tails start by being chestnut, but whiten with age.

Breeding is from any type of recognized light horse breeds, but the infusion of pony or draught blood is barred. The three main types are the Parade (or Show) type; the Bridle Path type, a general utility saddle-horse; and the Stock Horse for range work.

So far as the British Isles is concerned, not until recent years has any effort been made to foster the Palomino, and today the body which is concerned with its future is the British Palomino Horse Society. At varying times classes have been held for them at horse shows and they have appeared in parades. It is satisfactory to note, however, that today there is a marked advance in the number of Palominos to be found here, with the consequent added number of shows which welcome this attractive horse. Even more satisfactory is the fact that the conformation of the Palomino is greatly improved and the true colour more firmly fixed. There seems to be a good market for a horse which can claim, after all, that where colour is concerned, it stands unbeaten for beauty.

Breed Society : The British Palomino Society.

In the Percheron Horse we have one of the most popular draught horses to be found at work today, and its popularity extends far beyond France, where it originated, for it is renowned not only in Great Britain but in America and in Canada and other parts of the British Commonwealth.   Its many qualities have caused the breed to spread through many Continental countries, and of all heavy breeds it is perhaps the most widely dispersed through the world.

As is the case with so many, it is an admixture, based probably upon the working horse of Belgium and Northern France, where a strong, short-legged and active horse was the type required.   The actual credit for founding the Percheron Horse is due to a certain number of French farmers who, about 130 years ago, farmed a small area not more than perhaps 150 sq km (60 sq miles), the district being known as Le Perche, from which, of course, the horse takes its name. There is no doubt they produced an animal of outstanding qualities.

The horse is of low draught, having a short and compact body of tremendous depth, with quarters of outstanding size. Exceptionally short-legged, it carries great bone, and it is surprising that so heavy a horse can be so active, for that is indeed what it is, and it is claimed of the Percheron that for farming work it is a great saver of time in getting to its daily job. The fact that it is a good footed horse may be the result of having been worked on stone block roads; none but horses of good, hard, blue feet such as those possessed by the Percheron could stand up to that kind of work, and it has, with them, well-set joints and flat, flinty bone. The horse, of course, is clean-legged, that is, it is devoid of hair or 'feather'. Percherons are docile and very easily handled, and because of this they are easy to break, especially if they have been handled as foals.

Description The British Percheron is essentially a heavy-draught horse possessing great muscular development combined with style and activity. Should possess ample bone of good quality, and give a general impression of balance and power. Colour, grey or black only, with a minimum of white. Skin and coat of fine quality. Size, stallions not less than 16·3 hands and mares not less than 16·1 hands, but width and depth not to be sacrificed to height. Head, wide across eyes, which should be full and docile; ears medium in size and erect; deep cheek, curved on lower side, not long from eye to nose; intelligent expression.

Body strong, neck not short, stallions full arched crest, wide chest, deep well-laid shoulders; back strong and short; ribs wide and deep, deep at flank; hind-quarters of exceptional width and long from hips to tail, avoiding any suggestion of goose rump. Limbs short and strong and full second thighs, big knees and broad hocks; heavy flat bone, short cannons, pasterns of medium length, feet of reasonable size and good-quality hard blue horn. Limbs as clean and free from hair as possible. Action, straight, bold, with a long, free stride rather than short, snappy action. Hocks well flexed and kept close.

Little more need be said of this admirable breed. Its whole future is dependent upon the extent to which the heavy horse survives the onslaught of the internal combustion engine, and it may be that the breed will flourish in some countries (for the Percheron has travelled far afield) and decline in others. In this connection there is little enough evidence for an opinion to be formed as to whether the clean-legged horse (Percheron or Suffolk) has proved to be the *more suitable*, compared with the breeds carrying a heavy growth of hair on heels and legs (Shires and Clydesdales).

Breed Society: British Percheron Society.

The tale goes that the Persian horses descending from the Tarpan were known as a breed long centuries before Christ.   There is a theory which may be liberally discussed that Persian horses were ancestors of the Arabs, which finds a great justification in the looks and many characteristics common to both breeds.   We may safely say that the Persian horse was a typical oriental horse of great beauty, full of quality, high spirited, speedy and courageous, making an excellent war horse, much appreciated by Islamic warriors.

Today there are many different breeds in Persia: Persian Arab, the Turkoman horse, Shirazi horse (the Gulf Arab), the Kurdistan pony, the Karabakh, the Bokhara pony, the Jomud, and some Russian breeds such as Orlov Trotters, etc.

The Pinto, or Painted Horse, of America must be well known to all readers of Wild West stories, and the word, which is of Spanish derivation, has come to be applied to all those queerly marked black-and-white and bay- or brown-and-white horses which we know in this country as piebald and skewbald.

Examples of this peculiar colouring, which is the result of the combined action of albinism (whiteness), melanism (blackness) and erythema (redness) on the skin, are found all over the world and in most breeds of horses, but more especially in the primitive types, so it cannot be said that the Pinto is a breed in the strict sense of the word. It is a fact, however, that horses of this coloration are widely prevalent all over the North and South

American continents, and the modern Pinto is recognized as a distinctive American horse. In recent years a society has been formed in the United States called the Pinto Horse Society, with the general objects of gaining recognition for, and the improvement of, typical Pinto horses and ponies, to study and perpetuate the type, to go in for scientific breeding and to establish a register of Pinto horses.

There is no doubt that the 'painted' horse is most attractive and spectacular to look at, especially if the markings are produced in the best of any of the established types. Horses of this colouration have had a reputation the world over for toughness and endurance, and for that reason, with the added advantage of natural camouflage, were always favourites with the American Indian as war and ceremonial horses. They are now equally popular with the American riding public, and ranches in Canada and the United States are devoted solely to breeding them.

There are no physical features peculiar to the Pinto, except that most specimens appear to have thick necks and rather heavy shoulders, but the types of marking are interesting. There are two distinct patterns, known as Overo and Tobiano, the names derived from the Spanish, and are used in the Argentine by the Criollo (q.v.) Registry.

In Overo markings the white patches always originate from the belly and extend upwards. The back, mane and tail are generally dark; dark and white alternate on the legs, which are rarely all white. White faces and glass (blue) eyes are fairly prevalent. There is no fixed rule about the size of the patches.

The Tobiano pattern can be distinguished from

the Overo by the fact that it has no regular place of origin, white patches starting often from the back, and that the white and coloured areas are usually larger and nearly always solid rather than patchy. White legs are more often found, but the white face and glass eye are not so frequent. The dark patches in both cases are mostly black, brown and bay. Tobiano horses tend to be larger and heavier than the Overos. There is no limit to the size and shape of the markings, which certainly contribute to the charm and variety of this distinctive type of horse.

Breeding results show that the Pinto strain is very potent and will reproduce itself fairly constantly. Special classes for these horses have been introduced into American shows, and the accepted judging rule is 50 per cent. for markings and 50 per cent. for conformation and performance.

In the days when horse-dealers were found in great numbers in the British Isles, it was claimed by them that they could always sell an 'odd-coloured' horse, as it was called. The reason for this was that because of its often strange marking, and the vivid effect caused by the white background, the horse would always draw the attention of the public. In short it was, especially if put to a smart butcher's, baker's or other tradesman's cart, a very good advertisement. That market, and how very great it was, has been lost and will never be recovered. As a hack of the riding school type the horse is in demand but not for hunting, where its colour is looked upon as too noticeable.

These horses are bred by the Clementina (now G. Dimitrov) Stud Farm in Bulgaria, by mating local, improved Arabian and Anglo-Arab mares to Arabian and mainly Anglo-Arab stallions of the Hungarian Gidran type (*q.v.*).   In the initial period a group of Anglo-Arabian stallions, imported from the Strelets (*q.v.*) and other stud farms in Russia, was used.   The breed was mainly developed through the later importation of Hungarian Gidran stallions: in 1911 'Algy Gidran'; in 1917, 'Gidran 46/12' and 'Jockey'; 1924, 'Murat' and 'Balkan'; 1933, 'Pirin'; and 1938, 'Vihar'.   All these stallions, with the exception of 'Jockey', have established eight principal strains, of which one can be traced directly to the stallion 'Sivori', imported from the Strelets Stud Farm in Russia in 1898.   After a 15 to 20-year period of out-breeding, the breed was later consolidated by inbreeding. At present, with a view to further improvement of the equestrian events, mares are crossed with selected English Thoroughbred stallions.

Pleven foundation mares and stallions have retained much of the shapely beauty of the Arabians. They have a harmoniously developed body and dynamic movements. The average height of these horses is 15·3 hands. Over the past few years many Pleven jumpers have won distinction at international events.

The Poles have been renowned through history as great horse-lovers and great horse-breeders, with a pronounced individuality in their methods. One of their great authors wrote once: 'Having prayed to God for help, then a horse lover does his best in breeding his horses . . . and trusts more to his own experience than to books'. Their horses have always been in great demand throughout Europe, whatever the breed or period, and the Polish cavalry of the 17th century, mounted on the Polish horse, was almost invincible.

These horses had Eastern blood in them, Arab, Barb, Turkish, Persian, etc. The Arab, however, played an increasingly important role in Polish horse-breeding, and has held the highest place in the estimation of the Poles since the 16th century, when the Polish Sigismund II (Augustus) was the

only European ruler to have a royal stud of pure
Arabs, kept at Knyszyn. Arabian horses were,
however, certainly introduced earlier than that
during the many wars with the Turks and Tartars.

The oldest Arab studs in Poland were those of
Chrestowka and Szamrajowska, belonging to the
Sanguszko family. The former, known as the
Slawuta Stud, dated from 1506, and was re-
organized in 1791 by Jerome Sanguszko, who in
1803 sent the first horse-buying expedition from
Europe to Arabia, which returned in 1805 with
five stallions and one mare. A second expedition
in 1816, which was greatly indebted to an English
resident in Aleppo named Rawson, brought back
nine fine stallions, of which the best were 'Hajlan'
and 'Dzielf', and one mare.

Other Polish princely families, such as Potocki,
Rzewuski and Rozwadowski, also imported Arabs
periodically; and one Polish nobleman, Count
Rzewuski, lived in the desert and became a
legendary figure among the Bedouin.

To the student of good horses and therefore of
correct conformation, the Polish Arab left little to
be desired. Of a good front, with well set-back
shoulders, the horse would in the majority of cases
always show a strong-topped, short-backed and
deep-set body on short legs.

Breed Society: The Arab Horse Breeding
Association of Poland.

Apart from racing, the prime purpose of the Polish breeding of Thoroughbreds (*q.v.*) was to improve the native stock and to produce a good half-bred riding and working horse.

The nature of the country—the wide agricultural lands, type of soil, lack of good roads, and distances from railways—rendered the heavy-draught horse, such as the Percheron and Shire, almost useless. The need was for strong, lighter-weight animals of good blood and bone.

In Poland a Half-bred horse is one which has English Thoroughbred, Arab, or Anglo-Arab blood on at least one side of its pedigree. Half-bred stud books or registers are kept, and entry into them is very strictly controlled. It was during the period between the wars that the breeding of Half-breds was reconstructed on a highly selective basis, and some very good types were produced. The requirements of cavalry during that time, of course, played an important part in this development.

The type of Half-bred varies in different provinces of Poland, according to variations of soil, climate, strains of blood and the local needs. That of the Poznan and Pomeranian provinces was based on the English Thoroughbred and was a big-boned animal of good conformation and action, bred from stallions of the Raçot Stud with both local and German (Trakehner) brood mares. These provinces specialized in producing cavalry remounts. In 1938 the Raçot Stud had four Trakehner stallions, eighty-six brood mares and a hundred young stock. ·

The Kielce province bred a horse full of quality, and of about 15·2 hands, from Arab stock. The

Lublin Half-bred has English blood; while Warsaw and Lodz provinces produce both English and Anglo-Arab Half-breds.

The dominant factor in the breeding of Half-breds was the army, which bought a large number of horses every year. The specifications, most strictly adhered to, were: medium size, full of quality, near to the ground, well-ribbed, with deep girth, strong legs and good bone, and free action. Good temperament, courage, endurance and ability to 'do' well were also essential qualities.

Half-breds were also much used in agriculture, where they proved themselves as useful as in military service. Polish horsemen on Half-breds competed in shows and tests all over Europe, and at the Berlin Olympic Games of 1936 Poles were the only riders other than the Germans who rode horses bred in their own country.

It is not really possible to compare the Polish Half-bred with the English Part-bred Arabian, since the English product has, so far as the Arab Horse Society's Register is concerned, confined entries to horses and ponies of the riding type, whereas the Polish counterpart has leaned towards producing a not-too-heavy horse for agriculture. It is, moreover, unlikely that the English Society will do the same.

As a general commentary it can be said with assurance that the meticulous care shown by the Polish horse-breeders in producing the Polish Arab has been exemplified in the Polish Half-bred.

By the term 'Polish Thoroughbreds' is meant horses of pure English Thoroughbred stock as bred and developed in Poland. The first English Thoroughbreds were introduced into Poland early in the 19th century by four men in particular: Count A. Zamozski, E. Eberhard, F. Ursyn Niemcewicz, and, rather later than the first three but no less prominent, Count Krasinski.

The Polish Horse Racing Association, analogous to the Jockey Club of England, was formed in 1841; but breeding racehorses was an expensive hobby, and did not extend beyond the efforts of a few rich families until 1872, when economic conditions improved generally. The introduction of the totalisator to race meetings in 1879 contributed materially to the improved financial conditions and so to the wider development of Polish Thoroughbred breeding.

The most important studs during this period were: L. Grabouski's stud, founded in 1846 at Leczna and later transferred to Serniki; Jan Ursyn Niemcewicz's, at Stoki in 1850; Count L. Krasinski's, at Krasne in 1857; Count August Potocki's, at Jablonna in 1866; W. W. Mysyrowicz's, at Łoś in 1867; Baron L. Kronenburg's, at Brzeź; Jan and Edward Reszka's, at Borowno and Skrzydow in 1883; H. Block's, at Leczna in 1893; Prince Lubomirski's, at Kruszyna in 1895; and Michal Berson's, in Leszno in 1897.

All these studs were of a very high standard, thanks mainly to the good brood mares imported from England, France, Germany and Austria. One of the best known stallions in those days was 'Flying Fox', imported from England by E. Blanc, who paid 37,000 guineas for him.   He stood at Jardy at a fee of 10,000 francs.

Thoroughbreds bred in Poland ran with success all over Europe, notably in Russia at Moscow, Petrograd (now Leningrad) and Tsarskoe Selo, as well as Baden-Baden, Vienna and Hamburg.

In the 1890s a number of big private stables declined, and were replaced by training stables on English lines, which had in training large numbers of individually owned and bred horses.   After 1903 with the death of the great amateur promoters of Thoroughbred breeding, such as Ludwik Grabowski and Count Krasinski, the breeding of racehorses in Poland declined.   There was, however, a considerable revival after the First World War, through the efforts of Frederik Juriewicz, who was responsible for saving over 200 Thoroughbreds evacuated to Odessa at the beginning of that war.   One of these horses won the 'Derby' at Odessa in 1918.   In 1919 they were returned safely to Poland via Rumania.

A general description of the Polish Thoroughbred must necessarily be for practical purposes identical with that of the English Thoroughbred. To what extent the racehorse of Poland will again affect racing in Europe is entirely problematical. As is generally known, the racing Thoroughbred of France not only survived quite successfully the Second World War, but after the lapse of but a very few years from its cessation, was once again competing with the English racehorse with very considerable success, not only in France, but in England itself.   In the late 1970s Thoroughbred breeding in Poland has drastically declined.

The Polo Pony is a type rather than a breed. As long as the game of polo has existed so has the polo pony, ranging in height from about 12 to 13 hands in the 16th century to 15·2 to 16 hands in 1939, and in breed from the mountain ponies of the Himalayas, the Manipuris of Assam, to the Thoroughbred and near-Thoroughbred of England, U.S.A. and the Argentine as well as the Arab. All these variations of pony are still played somewhere or other, for the type of pony used depends on the local conditions and state of development of the game, and, though varying in degree, the requirements of the polo pony are practically the same in all cases.

Polo is a very ancient game, having been played

in the Far East, from Persia to Japan, for at least 2,000 years, the name being derived from the Tibetan word *pulu*, meaning a ball. The English naturally discovered it when they went to India, and it was brought back to England, and the first match was played at Hounslow in 1869, advertised as 'Hockey on Horseback'. The height of the ponies was then about 14 hands, and was stabilized by the Hurlingham Club in London (now at Loxwood, near Billinghurst in Sussex), which became the governing body of the game in 1873. The height of the pony steadily rose with the development of the game, was 14·2 hands before the First World War and was unlimited from 1919 onwards.

In the 'nineties of the last century greater interest was taken in the breeding of polo ponies, when various well-known and enthusiastic players in England began to breed from small thoroughbred sires on good foundation *pony* mares selected for *performance* on the polo ground. Their aim was to reproduce an animal based on pure pony blood which would have the quality and stamina of a miniature hunter, but which would be a true bred *pony*, not a small horse.

Sir Humphrey de Trafford's Thoroughbred pony 'Rosewater' is considered to be the foundation of the modern polo pony, and he had three famous sons: 'Sandiway', out of 'Cuddington'; 'Lord Polo', out of 'Lady Florence'; and 'Hurlingham', out of 'Esmeralda'. These three were dispersed to various studs and so widely disseminated the blood of 'Rosewater'.

The absolute criterion of a good polo pony is performance; any other standard alone is artificial. Some of the best polo ponies of the world in any age would never have got a prize in any show-ring. A polo pony has to be able to gallop at full speed, stop in its own length, turn or swing round, and start again at top speed in any direction. It has to be able to half passage at full gallop and to change leading leg at any speed or angle.

The chief characteristics of a polo pony therefore are: long neck, with plenty of room for flexion between the jaw and the junction of neck and head; good shoulders; short strong back and well-sprung ribs, with plenty of room for the lungs, elbows well away from the body, exceptionally powerful quarters, and hocks well let down; and, not least, a courageous, eager temperament.

The most optimistic supporter of polo in England could hardly have imagined the post-war revival of the game which has taken place. While it is abundantly clear that the pre-war standard of the pony itself has perhaps not been reached, any more than the amenities of extreme luxury associated with the game have returned, none the less the number of provincial clubs and private polo grounds opened has given the greatest satisfaction.

It is a quality in humans to strive for better things, and the best, if attainable. Where the difference between playing an indifferent pony and one of first-rate ability is so great, it can be assumed that many newcomers will be constantly acquiring ponies of better quality and higher training, which suggests that the future is favourable.

Breed Society: The National Pony Society.

Besides the excellent breed of Orlov Trotters, there are several other Russian breeds to be mentioned, such as the heavy-draught horse Bitjug, steppe horse of Russia, and the Viatka pony.

Russian saddle-horses, called also the Orlov Rostopchin breed, were formed from crossing the Orlov Trotter with the Rostopchin saddle-horse. The latter was bred from Arabs and English Thoroughbreds in the early 19th century by Count Rostopchin, a great Russian breeder, on his properties at Veronevo, near Moscow, and later in Orel and Veronej. At a later date his studs were bought by the Russian Government, and since then the Rostopchin saddle-horse has been crossed with the Orlov Trotter, giving as the result what is now called the Russian saddle-horse. In the Ukraine there were three breeding-centres of Russian saddle-horse in its pure type, but during the First World War they were looted by the Germans.

Later there were some serious attempts to restore the breed, and not without success. In *Animal Breeding Abstracts* (June 1946), A. Sokolov wrote:

It is hoped that the breed will have been restored in twenty to twenty-five years. The breeding plan envisages the creation of complex hybrids having 16/32, 7/32, 4/32, 2/32 and 1/32 blood of Russian saddle-horse, Arab, English Thoroughbred, Don, Russian Trotter and Akhal-Teké breeds respectively. The ultimate aim is to evolve a breed which will have 3/4, 1/8 and 1/6 blood of Russian saddle horse, Arab and English Thoroughbred respectively.

Steppe horses belong to a group of Mongolian horses descending from the Przevalsky horse, and have many varieties. All of them, however, represent the same type of small horse (13 to 14 hands) with a very strong constitution and a rather heavy, ugly head on a ewe neck. Their legs are very short, but strong and muscular, with small, hard hooves, while their thin coats are covered with very rich, coarse hair protecting them from the severity of the Russian climate. They are very hard and resist all kinds of privation, which is the natural result of being bred in the steppes and having to find under the snow only grass or moss to live on. They have great speed and stamina, and are great weight-carriers. In the past it was common to see a 15-stone Cossack galloping on a 13-hands pony. One remarkable achievement was the ride of Cossack D. Pieszkow, who covered nearly 9656 km (6,000 miles) in six months' riding on a steppe horse.

In modern times steppe horses have served as saddle-horses for many Mongolian tribes of Russia or as an agricultural horse for peasants. Later, to increase their size, steppe horses of Russia were crossed with English Thoroughbreds, giving in the result an animal from 14·1 to 14·3 hands. They are bred on natural pastures.

Many countries throughout the world have bred and adopted as their own the Thoroughbred horse, and such is its fame as a racehorse and usually so perfect its conformation that it is generally claimed as an established breed in those countries. Thus we have the Russian Thoroughbred which has been developed over a period of more than 200 years. The present century has seen the introduction of such famous Thoroughbred horses as 'Galtee More', which won the St. Leger, the Derby winners 'Minoru' and 'Aboyeur', the winner of the French Derby, 'Palmiste', and the Grand Prix winner, 'Quo Vadis', and a number of others.

For a description of the horse, reference should be made to the English Thoroughbred. Those horses bred in Russia can be expected to stand over 16 hands.

This term includes the 'Fjord Pony' of Norway, the Gudbrandsdal, another Norwegian indigenous breed, both of which have already been dealt with, and the native ponies of Sweden, Finland and the Baltic States.

In appearance and ancestry, so far as is known, they belong to that group of horses comprising the ponies of the British Isles and North-west Europe generally.   At the time when extensive animal migration seems to have been in progress, the British Isles were joined to Europe by land, which tends to support the idea of common origin.

The Finnish horse of today is of medium size, very agile and nimble-footed, with great staying power and toughness of constitution, good, hard feet and strong legs, body thick and muscular.   It is mainly used for draught in either wheeled carts or sleighs.

It is probable that the Swedish horse was originally introduced into the country from the Baltic regions from a type supposed to have originated in the Ukraine.   There have been found in Sweden the neck vertebrae of a prehistoric horse identical with the Russian Tarpan.   Besides this native animal, which varies very little from the Finnish pony, there are various cultivated breeds in Sweden which are considered separately.

Historically horses are not mentioned in Sweden until the 6th century, by which time the Swedes were renowned for their horses.   Generally the horse appears late in Scandinavia, as may be gathered from their mythology.   Thor, the most ancient of the northern gods, is never shown on horseback or in a chariot; the later deities, however, have taken to the horse, Odin on his eight-legged grey 'Sleipnir', Heimdal on a yellow-maned horse.

In Norway, in addition to the horse of the Fjords, there is an original type of island horse known as the Gudbrandsdal (*q.v.*), which was well-known in North Europe and has been one of the past founders of the modern Swedish breeds.   It is a larger animal than the Fjord horse and a good riding horse too.

In the Baltic States are horses of the same primitive types, notably the small Esthonian or Smudish (Zmudzin), the Zemaitukas (*q.v.*).   A Baltic derivative of these types is the Panje, which is a cross between native mares and trotter stallions, and is very popular as a riding and working horse. It ranges between 14 and 15 hands high, and has all the tough, enduring qualities of its ancient forbears, together with good temper and speed.

In reviewing this breed it is well to have in mind what has been written of the Fjord, the Gudbrandsdal and indeed any and all of the North European breeds, because of their close affinity, and in the main their original tap-root.

This horse is bred in the western part of
Schleswig Province. In the Middle Ages it was
much appreciated, as well as the Friesian, as a
saddle-horse to carry heavy armoured knights.
Since that time its breeding has been well patron-
ised by German rulers. At the end of the 19th
century the Schleswig Horse Breeders Association
was organized to control its breeding and produce
a type of horse which could be useful as both an
artillery horse and a heavy cart-horse. Schleswig
Province belonged at one time to Denmark, and
the breeding of the Schleswig and Jutland horse is
similar.

As one of the smallest breeds of ponies, the
Shetland is known throughout the whole of the
civilized world, and is remarkable for being probably the strongest member of the equine world in
relation to its size.   It is claimed that the Falabella
(*q.v.*), which is Shetland-bred, is the smallest pony
known.   The pony's origin is unknown, but
records of its existence in the Shetland Isles, lying
to the north of Scotland, date back many centuries.
Its diminutive size is thought to be due to the severe
climate of the regions where it lives, but this is not
entirely true, as generations of specimens bred in
the South of England and elsewhere seem to
increase little if anything in size.   In the islands
the pony certainly has much to endure, especially
at the end of a severe winter and before the spring

grass appears, and often has to rely on seaweed for its food.

Not until the middle of the 19th century was any attempt made in the way of selective breeding, and it was a few years prior to this that the pony was first used in the coal pits. Previously to that, its general use in the islands was, in spite of its size, as a saddle-pony and as a pack-pony, generally for carting seaweed for fertilizing the ground. The great demand from the pits caused the breeding of these ponies to flourish, and as the buyers took the best the stock became very poor in quality, until the 5th Marquis of Londonderry established a stud in 1870 in the Islands of Bressay and Noss. His stallion 'Jack' as a foundation sire became famous and has had a profound influence on the breed.

Owing to the growing number of mines which are now electrified, the demand for the pony has decreased in recent years and it has become increasingly evident that the pony's market is more that of a saddle-pony for children, for whom, owing to its docile and tractable character, it is well suited. Added to this, it has a picturesque and quaint beauty quite unlike any other breed. Withal, it is a lovable character and is deservedly popular, and much kept just as a pet.

Description Height average is 40 inches. Registered stock must not exceed 40 inches at three years old and 42 inches at four years old and over. Colour: black is the foundation colour, but can be bay, brown, chestnut, grey and parti-colours, etc. Coat changes according to the seasons of the year —double coat in winter and smooth in summer. Head, well-shaped and sensible-looking, and ears nicely placed, broad in forehead, with fairly straight fore face (not dish faced or roman nosed), sound mouth and pleasing eye (wall-eyes not favoured, especially in solid colours). Neck should rise off a well-laid oblique shoulder, strong and muscular, with good crest, especially in stallions. The length of neck should be in proportion to the size of the pony. Body, thick set and deep ribbed, with short back, broad chest and quarters, nice sloping shoulder, tail well set on, profuse mane and tail, and feathering of straight hair. Loins strong and muscular. Legs: forelegs well placed under the shoulder and chest, and standing plumb (not knock-kneed nor too wide apart) with well-muscled forearm, strong knees followed through by good flat bone (not back in the knee). Nice springy pasterns (not too short or long). Hind legs, thighs strong and muscular with broad, sharply developed hocks followed through by good flat bone and pasterns (not cow-hocked or wide behind). Feet, tough, round and well-shaped (not short, narrow, contracted or thin). Action, straight full movement, fore and hind, bending knees and hocks well sprung (not exaggerated or stilted).

Breed Society: The Shetland Pony Stud Book Society.

Both in height and weight the Shire horse is the largest of England's agricultural horses. At one time it was used to a considerable extent as a draught horse in all the large towns throughout the country. Properly the breed belongs to the Midlands and Fens of East Anglia.

The Shire traces its ancestry back to the Old Black English Carthorse of the 18th century and further back still to importations of black horses probably of Flemish origin.

It has often been wrongly stated that knights of the Middle Ages were mounted on these extremely heavy animals. This is not so, since the knight rode a stout, strong cob and in fact, no breed of really heavy horses was evolved or created until nearly two hundred years after the use of knight in armour ceased to be an element of warfare, owing to the invention of firearms.

In England the horse is bred largely in the deep and heavy-soiled counties of Lincoln and Cambridge, where its enormous strength makes it popular as an agricultural horse. The best of the breed stand over 17 hands and are capable of pulling a net weight of 5·08 t (5 tons), and although perhaps the slowest worker of the heavy breeds, the Shire is a steady, level mover of great honesty.

Bays and browns are the predominating colours, while blacks and greys are less frequent, and all Shires have a considerable amount of white on the feet and legs.

In character this great horse is of a docile nature, and at three years old it can be worked on the farms, soon becoming a commercial proposition. Representatives of the breed are to be found at most horse shows where agricultural classes are to be seen.

Description Colour: predominating colours bays and browns, then blacks and greys. Height, 16·2 to 17·3 hands; average about 17 hands. Head, lean in proportion to body, neither too large nor too small. Forehead, broad between the eyes. Eyes, large, prominent and docile in appearance. Nose: nostrils thin and wide, lips together and nose slightly roman. Ears, long, lean, sharp and sensitive. Throat, clean-cut and lean. Shoulders, deep and oblique and wide enough for the collar to rest on. Neck, fairly long, slightly arched, well set up to give the horse a commanding appearance.

Breed Society: The Shire Horse Society.

When the Saracens invaded Spain they brought with them a large number of Barb and Arab horses, which in consequence greatly improved the native stock. The crossing of Spanish horses with Barbs and Arabs resulted in the Spanish Ginete, famous for its beauty, great docility and obedience. Their main characteristics were a great width of breast, powerful shoulders, roman noses, long arched neck with full and flowing mane, goose rumps, and rather extravagant high action so much appreciated later on in the Vienna School, where they excelled at the traditional 'artificial airs'.

This proud, showy action and splendid appearance recommended them for studs in Austria and Italy, where special breeds were created such as Kladruber, Lipizzaner and the Neapolitan horse which was used for parades.

The Spanish Ginete described by Richard

Berenger (d. 1782) as 'docile and affectionate to man yet full of spirit and courage' deserved the highest praise from William Cavendish, 1st Duke of Newcastle in *A New Method and Extraordinary Invention to Dress Horses* (1667):

. . . if well-chosen, is the noblest horse in the world . . . the most beautiful that can be, for he is not so thin and lady-like as the Barb, nor so gross as the Neapolitan. He is of great spirit and of great courage and docile, hath the proudest walk, the proudest trot and the best action in his trot; the loftiest gallop, the swiftest careers and is the lovingest and gentlest horse and fittest of all for a King in day of Triumph . . . much more intelligent than even the best Italian horses, and for that reason the easiest dressed, because they observe too much with their eyes, and their memories are too good.

They made 'absolutely the best stallions in the world to breed horses for War, Manège, Ambling pad-horses, and for running horses'.

The best Spanish Ginetes were bred in the Spanish Royal Stud at Cordova and are supposed to descend from the Barb stallion called 'The Cusman' and Andalusian mares.

Later, the Spanish horses degenerated considerably, except the Andalusian breed (*q.v.*) which goes back to the Middle Ages and carries much Arabian and Barb blood, and which in the past provided a large proportion of army remounts. Today the most important stud in Spain is at Jerez, where are bred 'warm-blood' horses.

Anyone who has travelled in Kashmir, Ladakh or towards the borders of Nepal will be familiar with the sight of long strings of pack-ponies plodding patiently and securely under huge loads up and down the narrow, dizzy paths of the Himalayas, with the characteristic short, quick step, head down and apparently half asleep, but always on the alert to nip somebody or something. He will probably have used them himself for carrying his own kit and will have ridden them—and once you have ridden a hill pony of the Himalayas you do not easily forget it, especially that terrifying habit they all have of keeping always to the extreme edge of a mountain path, so that one leg dangles over several hundred feet of nothingness. The reason for this is, of course, the fact that the animal is used to carrying a wide pack on either side of its body, so it keeps to the outside of a track to avoid bumping against the cliff wall on the inner side.

The general characteristics of the hill pony, whose origin is certainly Mongolian, are the same all over the Himalayas and the highlands of Central Asia, but there are two characteristic breeds in India, the Spiti and the Bhutia, which it is convenient to deal with together. The former takes its name from the Spiti tract, a very mountainous region which lies in the Kangra District between Kulu, where the apples come from, and the central spine of the Himalayas. The breeding of these animals is one of the main sources of income of the inhabitants, who do a good trade in them with the surrounding hill districts and states, extending even into Tibet. The breeding is mainly in the hands of one tribe, Kanyats, who are high caste Hindus, and is carried out in small units of two or three, and never more than six mares. The Kanyats are very proud of their hereditary calling, and claim to be able to distinguish representatives of this breed in any unknown drove of ordinary hill ponies.

Mares usually have their first foal at four years, and March and April are the foaling months. Very little attention is paid to the care of mares and foals, and they live on what they can pick up on the mountainsides. Inbreeding is practised to keep down the size, and breeding is usually from parent to progeny rather than from brother to sister.

The Spiti is small, tough, thickset, up to plenty of weight and very sure-footed. It has an intelligent head with remarkably sharp ears, strong, short back, short legs with good bone, and hard round feet. The neck is short and thick, tapering slightly towards the head; the shoulders are sturdy and straightish, the ribs well sprung and quarters well developed. It thrives only in the cold heights of the Himalayas, and in spite of its hard life it is full of character and humour, and is tireless and apparently indestructible.

The Bhutia pony is bred in parts of Nepal and other Himalayan regions from the Punjab to Darjeeling. It has much the same characteristics as the Spiti, except that it is slightly bigger, averaging 13 to 13·2 hands as against the 12 hands of the latter. The predominant colours of both breeds are grey and iron grey.

This is the official name of the famous American trotting and pacing horses. Harness racing, whether trotting or pacing (which is the lateral movement as opposed to the diagonal), may be said to hold pride of place in popularity as a horse spectacle with the American public; and these animals are bred and trained with extreme care and with truly American scientific efficiency.

The father of the modern Standard trotter was Rysdyk's 'Hambletonian', also known as 'Hambletonian 10' from his Standard number in the register. Foaled in 1849, he descended in three ways (direct male line and two collateral crosses) from the English Thoroughbred 'Messenger', the *fons et origo* of all American trotting horses, who, himself was the son of the Thoroughbred

'Mambrino'. And through him the breed goes back in the male line, through 'Blaze', to the Darley Arabian. Allied with this principal foundation element are many other Thoroughbred strains, and also Morgan, Norfolk Trotter and other light horse strains. The Norfolk Trotter 'Bellfounder' was imported into America in 1788.

The Standard Bred trotter breed dates officially from 1879, when the National Association of Trotting Horse Breeders adopted a set of rules for admission to the American Trotting Register (first published in 1871) based on speed. The rules have been varied from time to time according to the great progress made in the establishment of the type, and now the Standard, from being largely one of performance and speed on the race track, is one of blood only. Selective breeding under the Standard has transformed an initially composite type into a homogeneous and firmly established one, renowned the world over; and the trotting horses of Europe all owe something to the American breed.

The characteristics of the breed are generally Thoroughbred, with modifications due to differences in gait and work. In the main the Standard Bred is heavier-limbed and more robustly built than the Thoroughbred, with longer body, shorter legs and greater endurance. The average height is 15·2 hands; 16 hands is seldom reached, while 15 hands is usually the lower limit. The weight in racing condition is 408 to 453 kg (900 lb to 1,000 lb). The horse possesses unequalled heart and stamina, which enable it to run heat after heat at top speed without flagging.

Breed Society: The United States Trotting Association.

The study of the breeds of Russian horses compared with those of most continental countries, particularly Germany and Austria, emphasizes the fact that so many breeds of these owe their existence, and certainly their development, to individual effort. Many well-known breeds have been created at certain large studs and indeed have taken the name of the stud as their breed-name. Examples of this can be found of course in other parts of the world. In Britain, however, the naming of breeds is entirely territorial, if we except the Percheron (*q.v.*), which, though firmly established here, is of French breeding. The Russian Strelets is an instance of stud-naming.

This horse is numbered among the more aristocratic of the Russian breeds of horses and might fairly be called with truth the Russian Arab. The source from which this good breed was built was in native mares from the mountainous regions of the Ukraine; these were the foundation stock of the stud, and the selected of them were then crossed with Anglo-Arab, Turkish, Persian or pure Arab sires. The progeny of these—the Strelets—are now breeding true to type. This breed can be described as a large Arab, with all the excellent attributes of that ancient race, and is unaffected apparently in spite of being bred for greater size. It is much admired as a supreme riding horse and is particularly valuable for cavalry needs.

One outstanding characteristic of the Suffolk
Horse, which is also known as the Suffolk Punch,
is that it is *always* chestnut in colour. No other
colour is seen, and if it were, would not be tolerated.
Furthermore, it shares distinctiveness with the
British Percheron of being the only clean-legged
British draught horse. It is indigenous to the
County of Suffolk on the eastern side of England,
and, according to Camden's *Britannia*, the
Suffolk Horse dates back to 1506. A curious
feature in connection with this breed is that every
specimen of the breed now in existence traces its
descent in direct male line in an unbroken chain to
a horse foaled in 1760.

It is unnecessary to point out that the Suffolk

has varied since those early days by the infusion of blood from certain strains possessed of a finer fore-hand, greater activity and perhaps a more elegant conformation. All this has produced what is now a very handsome horse with a fine record of per-formance, for the Suffolk will work well as a two-year-old and go on until it is in the mid-twenties, and withal it is a very economical horse to keep, doing well on little and poor feed at that. It should be mentioned that, with rare exceptions, it is very docile.

In height it stands about 16 hands, and, unlike the Clydesdale, it should have great width in front and in the quarters. Another feature of the horse is its short legs and consequent low draught, giving great direct pull on its vehicle. Its great body is a feature, and the horse is possessed of a round and friendly yet impressive appearance which is very marked. The fact that it can, if asked, trot in a way which can hardly be expected of the Shires and Clydesdales, is claimed in its favour. Old records in the form of advertisements show that many matches were held in pulling contests in the County of Suffolk, which would seem to show that the great strength of the Suffolk, even in those days, was well recognized.

Much has been said and written in years past of the supposed unsoundness of the feet of the Suffolk, and it is generally accepted that there was then real foundation for this. It can be stated, however, that it is many years since breeders have had to consider this real defect, and the Suffolk is now a sound-footed animal.

Description Colour, chestnut, a star or a little white on face is no detriment. Head, big, with broad forehead. Neck, deep in collar, tapering gracefully towards the setting of the head. Shoulders, long and muscular, well thrown back at wither. Body, deep, round ribbed from shoulder to flank, with graceful outline in back, loin and hind-quarters; wide in front and behind; the tail well up with good second thighs. Feet, joints and legs: the legs should be straight with fair sloping pasterns, big knees and long clean hocks on short cannon-bones free from coarse hair. Elbows turned in regarded as a serious defect. Feet having plenty of size with circular form protecting the frog. Walk and trot, smart and true, with well-balanced and good action.

With so admirable a foundation it is not surprising that efforts have been made by many to cross the Suffolk with Thoroughbreds and Arabs in the endeavour to evolve heavy-weight hunters and cobs. These attempts in general have met with varying success, as must always be the case with such a contrasting out-cross. None the less many good specimens have been produced which have from time to time evoked great enthusiasm. Cross-breeding of this nature, however, must always carry with it an abnormal degree of chance.

Breed Society: The Suffolk Horse Society.

Besides the native pony type already described
(see Scandinavian) there is in Sweden a general
utility type of horse, the result of crosses between
the local 'cold-blooded' horses of the north and
west of Europe and the 'warm-blooded' animals
from the East, the latter blood not direct but
through various European breeds. These in
recent times have been mainly Anglo-Norman and
Trakehner stallions, which have introduced
Thoroughbred strains into the native stock and
considerably improved the breed.

The resulting type is a compromise between ride
and draught, the army demanding remounts more
and more Thoroughbred in character and agriculture requiring heavier and stronger animals for
farm work. In general this type is a 'warm-

blooded' horse, strong, compact, with short clean legs and a good temperament, useful for both saddle and draught.

In Northern Sweden there is a special type of draught horse, known as the North Swedish Horse. Earlier attempts to establish the breed had failed, but in 1900 an association was formed with the object of creating the North Swedish Horse. The method was a steady grading-up of the existing local stock by crosses to Gudbrandsdals from Norway (see Scandinavian), and proved successful. In 1944 there were 400 stallions in service to about 15,000 mares a year, producing some 8,000 pure North Swedish horses annually. By then the importation of Gudbrandsdal had practically stopped, but the Oldenburg (*q.v.*) was being imported in increasing numbers. The North Swedish Horse is eminently suited to light-draught agricultural work in Northern Sweden.

The most popular heavy-draught horse in Sweden is the Swedish Ardennes, comprising more than 60 per cent of the country's horse stock. The Ardennes (*q.v.*) were first introduced from Belgium in 1837 before they had been crossed with the heavier Brabant. In 1901 a Stud Book was opened for the breed, and since 1924 the Breeding Association for the Swedish Ardennes Horse has kept pedigrees and registered all foals.

In 1950 a horse census in Sweden showed the number of horses of all ages to be 439,760. Of these about 16,000 were 'warm-blood' horses, 138,000 'cold-blood' light-draught, and 286,000 'cold-blood' heavy-draught. An unofficial count, made in 1970, recorded a total of 60,652 horses of all types.

Much confusion exists about this very ancient strain of wild horses who contributed to the ancestry of most European and some Eastern breeds of horses and ponies. The forest Tarpan: *Equus przevalskii gmelini* Antonius once roamed the forests of central and eastern Europe, whilst the steppe Tarpan was found in herds south of the Ural mountains.

These animals were hunted extensively and practically to extinction. In the late 18th century a few survivors were kept in reserves such as that of Count Zamoyski in Poland and in the Bialowiecz Forest.

In the vast and isolated regions of Eastern Europe undoubtedly the small peasant farmers had always caught up wild Tarpans and had domesticated them. During the unusually cold winter of 1808 when fodder was extremely scarce, those wild Tarpans in the Zamoyski reserve were caught and distributed amongst the peasants of neighbouring villages, and others from the Bialowiecz herd were also distributed. This was the last act of domestication of wild horses in Poland. Small primitive horses with the conformation colour and other characteristics similar to those of their ancestors the wild Tarpans survived with the peasants in the forests and backward areas around Zamoyski's reserve until the end of World War II.

In the course of his studies on primitive horses Prof. T. Vetulani decided to regenerate the forest Tarpan with the help of these animals. These were collected and taken to a special reserve in Bialowiecz Forest in 1936 where they were kept in wild conditions, with additional hay only in winter. In 1939 there were three stallions, thirteen mares and nineteen foals. A number perished during the Second World War. In 1955 all the animals were transferred to the reserve at Popiellno (where this photograph was taken). Popiellno lies deep in the forest on the great Sperding lake. The environmental conditions are particularly favourable and two herds now live natural lives without shelter or veterinary attention, whilst a domesticated herd is kept at the Science Centre for special study into freedom from disease.

Many generations have now survived and increased and the forest Tarpan is once more to be found living the life of a wild horse. The coat colour is generally mouse dun or blue dun with some striping on the legs, and sometimes striping on the entire body. Black mane and tail and a black dorsal stripe is common to all animals. In winter some grow a longer whiter coat.

Although the official name of this horse is the Tennessee, it is better and more popularly known in America as the Plantation Walking Horse, which indicates the special purpose for which it was produced, to carry the farmers and planters of the South at a comfortable pace over their plantations. Like the Morgan Horse (*q.v.*), this breed owes its foundation to one powerful prepotent stallion (known as 'Black Allan', from his colour) a Standard Bred trotting stallion of mixed Hambletonian and Morgan ancestry. Foaled in 1886, he was taken to Tennessee as a colt, and like 'Justin Morgan', the progenitor of the Morgan breed, had a long life at stud and produced numerous progeny, mainly from the Tennessee mares of mixed

Thoroughbred, pacing and saddle-horse strains. He was a sire of great prepotency, reproducing his type regularly and carrying on the blood with all its power in succeeding generations with constant uniformity. The breed was a natural production from the needs of the place and times, and established itself as a most popular and useful type purely on its own merits.

The Walking Horse is a much heavier and more powerful animal than the American Saddle Horse (q.v.), and is generally larger, stouter, more robust and less elegant than the latter. The head is large and plain, neck rather short, body and quarters solid and massive, with heavier limbs. The prevailing colours are bay, black and chestnut, while roan is common and greys are also found. It is temperate by disposition, intelligent and well-mannered. Its principal characteristic, from which it derives its name, Walking Horse, is the running walk, fast, easy and enduring, the gait which is so much favoured by the Southern planters and farmers. Careful training is needed to develop the true running gait, which is liable to turn into the 'pace' if pressed.

In addition, it also has other paces: a good ordinary walk; it canters well; and is a good trotter in harness. Members of this breed have for a long time been widely used for agricultural work on farms, as well as for riding, and are undoubtedly first-class general-purpose animals, useful on the farm, between the shafts, or under saddle. In weight it runs to 453 kg (1,000 lb) and over, and in height is seldom below 15·2 hands.

Breed Society: The Tennessee Walking Horse Breeders' Association of America.

These horses are bred and developed in the Stavropol region (North Caucasus) of the U.S.S.R. as the result of crossing Russian Arab stallions (Strelets, *q.v.*) with pure-bred Arabian and Kabarda mares (*q.v.*). Tersk horses are good natured, agile, good movers, and are capable of considerable endurance.

As can be readily assumed from its breeding, the Tersk horse shows many characteristics of the Arab horse background which is evidenced by its shoulder, rather flat wither, very short back and generous flat croup. With its over-all quality it is a true saddle-horse, averaging about 15 hands in height.

The name is synonymous with the present-day racehorse, and the Thoroughbred is the best-known of all British breeds, famous throughout the world, and to a large extent represents all that is best in the horse world; indeed the Thoroughbred sets a degree of excellence in points which has become a standard.

All Thoroughbreds trace their ancestry to three eastern sires, and their names are well known—the Darley Arabian, the Godolphin Barb and the Byerley Turk. Much has been written to suggest that these famous horses were put to English mares, but, on the other hand, there is much evidence to suggest that some of the foundation mares were Eastern mares. As time went on, less and still less Arab blood was introduced, and the desire for more speed became paramount and more insistent, for today the Arab cannot live with the Thoroughbred in any test of speed, for the latter has become truly a racing machine, and a very wonderful one at that. Even now times tend to become even faster and as a result the price of racing stock escalates.

The value of the breed, therefore, being based almost entirely on speed, those which cannot win on the racecourse tend to become of little value, unless possessed of some admixture in their breeding which is particularly sought after. The great majority of the horses are gelded, and they and the mares find a market among those seeking hunters, hacks and even polo ponies. Latterly the market for unwanted Thoroughbred mares has become somewhat more 'open' to cross with the Arab, producing as they do a most desirable animal in the Anglo-Arab (q.v.), often an animal of exceptional beauty, with a more equable temperament than the Thoroughbred. The Thoroughbred is much used as a sire to produce hunters.

The Thoroughbred at its best is a very beautiful horse, perhaps the most beautiful in the world, with the exception of the Arab. It must be stated, however, that as the result of a number of contributory causes, much unsoundness in wind and limb exists.

A *description* of the horse must be that of the highest class of light horse in existence. The head refined, the neck elegant and arched, withers pronounced, and the shoulder very sloping; legs, clean, hard and of good bone with tendons pronounced. The back short, the body deep with ribs well-sprung to barrel shape, the croup high. Tail well set and quarters generous to a degree with hocks well let down, standing true and moving with a great striding action. The whole, one of intense refinement and indicative of great speed.

The position of the Thoroughbred in the world of horses is an enviable one for two very potent reasons. Flat-racing and steeplechasing are so firmly established, constituting now almost a national industry, that it seems inconceivable that any elimination or marked reduction in the sport need be feared. No other breed of horse can ever take the place of the Thoroughbred on account of its speed, even if any other breed were made eligible for entry at Weatherby and Sons, which again is inconceivable. The breed stands unchallenged as a racehorse.

The preceding pages have shown repeatedly that the Thoroughbred, along with the Arab, is the main source of up-grading of very many breeds. As this has been practised for centuries it may be fairly assumed that its value is proved beyond possibility of doubt.

The Jockey Club is the body controlling flat-racing in England.

This pony is of good repute in Australia and
New Zealand, and has always been well used in
harness and under saddle. It is also to be seen at
times in the show ring. Although permitted,
colours are not defined—indeed it seems the breed
is found in any colour—it is interesting that such
an attractive admixture frequently occurs as chocolate body, cream spots and cream mane and tail,
suggesting the Appaloosa type. The ideal pony is
one of good girth, strong across the back and
quarters. These Timor ponies are eager, sure-
footed and tireless, and possessed of considerable
natural wisdom. Because of this they are largely
used for stock work, for which they are admirably
suited, since quite heavy weights seem to trouble
them not at all. They originate from the Island of
Timor, Indonesia.

Undoubtedly the best German breed is the East-Prussian horse. East Prussia, the biggest horse-breeding centre of the German Reich before the end of the Second World War, used to supply to the German Army the largest number of remounts, while before the war breeding East Prussian foals and selling them as yearlings was an extremely profitable proposition for local farmers.

The most prominent role in the foundation of the East Prussian breed was played by the Trakehnen Stud, founded in 1732 by Frederick William I of Prussia (father of Frederick the Great), who supplied both the land and the foundation breeding material, partly from Royal Studs and partly by importation of many high-class Arabs from Prince Radziwill's Stud at Taurogi, in Poland. Trakehner horses soon became the pride of German horse-breeding, and the Trakehnen Stud became the Newmarket of the East Prussian breed.

The Trakehnen Stud, which had a 200-year-old tradition and more, lay in the north-east part of East Prussia and, looking at the beautifully drained plains with excellent pastures well supplied with lime and phosphorus to give horses good bone, one could hardly believe that in the first quarter of the 18th century the same place was swampy and only covered by shrubs. The stud is now in ruins since the surrounding country was devastated by Soviet troops.

The Trakehner horse is a beautiful and good-tempered animal, well ribbed, standing about 16 hands, with strong back and having a very good action. The horse comes of local and Schweiken origin, the breed graded up by Arabs and English Thoroughbreds of heavier type.

In the Trakehnen Stud the service period was towards the end of November and foals were left with their dams until four and a half months old. As three-year-olds they were sent to the training establishment, which was on the spot, where they remained for a year. When they were four-year-olds they were submitted to trials which included hunting with a pack of hounds and cross-country races, the obstacles being fences, banks and open ditches. The best were retained for breeding in the Trakehnen Stud, the second best went to State studs, the third class being sold to private breeders. These three classes were branded with double elk-antlers on the nearside thigh, while those who did not pass the tests were castrated and sent as remounts to the army. The important role in improvement of the Trakehner horse was played by the stallion 'Perfectionist' by 'Persimmon' out of 'Perfect Dream of Morion'. The best offspring during World War I were those of the stallions 'Persival' and 'Dampfross von Dingo'. The association of breeders of light horse of Trakehner origin counted 10,000 members with 20,000 mares registered, while four State studs bred army remounts in East Prussia from 500 stallions and 33,000 mares.

From the foregoing it will be seen that this famous breed has been fostered with characteristic German thoroughness, for it is doubtful whether any organized breeding has insisted on such exhaustive training as was undertaken at the Trakehnen Stud. It is hard to imagine, too, an association watching over the interests of one breed of light horse claiming a membership of 10,000. This is a tribute to the breed, which has always been held in high esteem by horsemen of many nations. No doubt the high quality, sound constitution and stamina of the breed owes something to Thoroughbred and Arab blood. The Trakehnen Stud was destroyed during the Second World War, but the breed is extensively fostered in the southern part of East Prussia, now belonging to Poland. The identical animal is bred in large numbers in Western Germany and is known by its old name of East Prussian, which breed is identical with the Trakehner.

Height, 16 to 16·2 hands.

The first named horse belongs to the native breeds of Turkey and is a descendant of the Turkmene of the central Asiatic steppes. There has always been a stream of imported horses into Anatolia or Turkey as the country is now called, since historically the country did not support a native breed as such. The Turkmene horse was undoubtedly known in England in the 16th century, and as some indication of the horse let us quote Thomas Blundeville who, in 1580, wrote of the Turk that they 'be indifferent faire to the eie, though not very great nor strong made, yet verie light and swift in their running and of great courage'. From this happily chosen word-picture it would appear that the horse was somewhat similar to the Barb.

As is well known, the famous 'Byerley Turk'

was imported into England in 1689, though certain authorities have asserted that he was not a Turk but an Arab. The 'Lister Turk', was imported by the Duke of Berwick in the reign of James II, while between the years 1690 and 1700 two horses, whose stock subsequently stamped their worth in a long line of racehorses, themselves achieved fame on the English Turf; they were imported by Lord D'Arcy—the 'White Turk' and the 'Yellow Turk'. In fact, no less than 32 Eastern sires of Turkmene origin appear in the pedigrees of the world-famous Thoroughbred horse (see J. Osborne, *The Horse-breeders Handbook*).

The most typically indigenous horses in Turkey are the Kurdistan ponies bred near Sivas. There it is the custom to cross the native mares with Arab stallions, thus encouraging a general grading-up of the native breed and turning out a good type of small working pony of 14 to 14·2 hands and well suited to native requirements. The Kurdistan is of the same root stock as the Turkoman and they have coarse heads, thick necks, short bodies and good bone. As may be supposed from their breeding, they are immensely hardy and greatly enduring, while in colour they are usually grey or bay.

The Ukranian saddle-horse has been developed
at the stud farm of the Ukraine, U.S.S.R., in the
same manner as English Hunters.   Large mares
of the West European saddle-horses were mated
with Thoroughbred stallions.   This has resulted
in a horse with exceptionally short legs showing a
wealth of bone, a strong body with a well-shaped
back, good girth and 'riding' shoulders.   It is a
well-proportioned animal and potentially a good
hunter, capable of carrying plenty of weight.   It
is claimed for the Ukrainian that it shows considerable jumping ability.

This breed, also known as the *Demi-sang de l'Ouest*, dates back to the early 17th century when the mares of Charente and Vendée were crossed with imports from Holland. Subsequent cross-breeding with Norman and Anglo-Norman, alternating with English Thoroughbred, Arab, Anglo-Arab and Norfolk blood went a long way towards up-grading the breed. Though by 1920 it was a fixed breed, like the product of Normandy, the crossing with Anglo-Norman studs continued. Bred and raised in Vendée, Deux-Sèvres, Charente, Charente Maritime and Vienne, its most distinguished and spirited specimens are found in the *Bocage Vendéen*, the foremost stud farms at La Roche-sur-Yon, Saintes and Angers. A fine saddle and draught horse, it has in the past served well as a cavalry and artillery horse.

Usually of large and sturdy build, it stands from 15 to 17 hands, has a high and deep chest, a powerful, well-set-on neck and rather long heavy parotid head. The top line of the body is good, with exceedingly fine withers, clearly defined and well back. The shoulder is long and well oriented, the legs sturdy and of good formation, the feet (a consequence of marsh-breeding) rather broad and flat. This breed, like the other half-breds raised in France, is nowadays known in that country under the name of *Cheval de Selle Français*.

The Viatka pony is native to the Baltic states and has Klepper blood. The colour is usually palomino, dun or chestnut with a dorsal stripe, and it is therefore one of the more primitive breeds of eastern European ponies. In outlook and conformation, the Viatka is not unlike the Konik (*q.v.*). Somewhat long in the back, they possess strong short legs, deep chests, well-sprung ribs; and their small heads, usually with a concave profile, are pleasantly 'breedy', although the lower jaw is often massive. Some have great speed. In winter they develop an immense coat and a subcutaneous layer of fat as a protection against the extreme cold. Varieties, named after their local provinces, are Obvinkas and Kazankas, around 13 hands.

The Welsh Cob is popular far beyond the confines
of Great Britain, for it is an animal of many virtues
and of outstanding strength and activity.   As a
breed it derives from the Welsh Mountain Pony,
whose antiquity dates from long before any true
records existed.

The Welsh Cob has had a great influence upon
trotting animals in many countries, and its blood
has gone far in the making of the outstanding
Hackney horse and pony of Great Britain.   It
was, too, very many years ago, used in the development of the Fell Pony, which up to comparatively
recent years has been used as a trotting pony.

As may be expected, the Welsh Cob has inherited much of the hardiness of the mountain
pony, which it resembles in many respects, for it
should have the same small head showing a lot of

quality, and the small, prick ears so characteristic of the pony. It must, too, have a strong, deeply girthed body and immensely powerful quarters with well-set-up tail, while its legs must be short and strong, standing over not too much ground and showing a broad and generous chest. In action it must be active and not show too much knee, and have with it a bold and virile carriage. Its uses are many and it can be described as the utility type. Few animals could be found more useful to the small farmer, for it is of a tractable nature and it is useful for all kinds of harness work, being capable of pulling a big weight and trotting on in a way to eat up the ground.

Welsh Pony (cob type) and the Welsh Cob (Section C and D of the Stud Book respectively)

General character: strong, hardy and active, with pony character and as much substance as possible. Colour: any colour, except piebald or skewbald. Head, full of quality and pony character. A coarse head and roman nose are most objectionable. Eyes, bold, prominent and set widely apart. Ears, neat and well set. Neck, lengthy and well carried. Moderately lean in the case of mares, but inclined to be cresty in the case of mature stallions. Shoulders, strong but well laid back. Forelegs, set square and not tied in at the elbows. Long, strong forearms; knees, well developed with an abundance of bone below them; pasterns, of proportionate slope and length; feet, well-shaped; hoofs, dense. When in the rough, a moderate quantity of silky feather is not objected to, but coarse, wiry hair is a definite objection. Middle-piece back and loins, muscular, strong and well coupled. Deep through the heart and well-ribbed up. Hindquarters lengthy and strong. Ragged or drooping quarters are objectionable. Tail well set on. Hindlegs: second thighs, strong and muscular, hocks, large, flat and clean, with points prominent, turning neither inwards nor outwards. The hindlegs must not be too bent and the hock not set behind a line falling from the point of the quarter to the fetlock joint; pasterns, of proportionate slope and length; feet well-shaped; hoofs, dense. Action, free, true and forceful. The knee should be bent and the whole foreleg should be extended straight from the shoulder and as far forward as possible in the trot. Hocks flexed under the body with straight and powerful leverage.

As an indication of type hardiness and stamina it should be noted that in the pre-mechanized army days, the cob, being capable of bearing an enormous weight, was much used for military pack work and for mounted infantry. Because of this, stallions of the right type were always in demand by foreign governments for the purpose of infusing the right blood and for the production of the right type of horses for army purposes.

In contemplating the future of the Welsh Cob of draught type and that of riding type, one can only conclude that the latter will retain its popularity in these days when any good riding horse is in such demand. It is interesting to reflect and to record the fact that in the Cob and the Mountain Pony the Welsh have two quite outstanding examples of horse-flesh.

Breed Society: The Welsh Pony and Cob Society.

One of the most popular and thought by most
people to be the most beautiful of Britain's mountain and moorland ponies, the Welsh Mountain
Pony, shown above, claims an existence so remote
as to be incalculable.   It is truly indigenous to the
soil it has so long graced and on which it has thrived
so well, in spite of the great hardships it has
endured with the passing of the seasons.   Today it
is still there, on the Welsh mountains and wastes,
wild or semi-wild, but always a potential joy to a
riding child or to the small tradesman as an honest
little worker between the shafts.   The very nature
of its ancestry and upbringing gives it those priceless qualities of intelligence, pluck, soundness and
endurance for which it is so justly famed.

The Welsh Mountain Pony, though so small in

height, performs really remarkable feats of strength and endurance, for it carries full-grown men without any apparent effort and certainly with no ill-effects. As a children's riding-pony it is very prominent, very popular and in the show-ring is most successful. The classic beauty of its head and the gay carriage of its tail, coupled with the generous centre-piece and quarters, give it an advantage over most other breeds.

It is claimed for the breed that the native pony mares of Wales had much to do with the breeding, in the very early days of the English Thoroughbred. It is at least certain, however, that the pony was much used for producing the polo pony, the Hackney and the Hunter, and, by no means the least important, the hardy, active and gay Welsh Cob.

The ponies are to be found fairly well scattered throughout the less populated parts of Wales. Owing to their small stature, they have in the past been in great demand in the coal-mines, but with the growing increase in mechanization, the demand is more now for children's riding-ponies.

Welsh Mountain Not exceeding 12 hands. (Section A of the Stud Book)

General characteristics: hardy, spirited and pony-like. Colour: any colour, except piebald or skewbald. Head, small, clean-cut, well set on and tapering to the muzzle. Eyes, bold. Ears, well-placed, small and pointed, well up on the head, proportionately close. Nostrils, prominent and open. Jaws and throat, clean and finely cut, with ample room at the angle of the jaw. Neck, lengthy, well-carried and moderately clean in the case of mares, but inclined to be cresty in the case of matured stallions. Shoulders, long and sloping well back. Withers, moderately fine. The humerus upright so that the foreleg is not set in under the body. Forelegs, set square and true, and not tied in at the elbows; long strong forearms; well-developed knee, short flat bone below knee; pasterns, of proportionate slope and length; feet, well shaped and round; hoofs, dense. Back and loins, muscular, strong and well coupled. Girth, deep. Ribs, well sprung. Hind-quarters, lengthy and fine. Not cobby, ragged or goose-rumped. Tail, well set on and carried gaily. Hindlegs, hocks to be large, flat and clean with points prominent, to turn neither inwards nor outwards; the hind leg not to be too bent; the hock not to be set behind a line from the point of the quarter to the fetlock joint; pasterns, of proportionate slope and length; feet well-shaped; hoofs, dense. Action, quick, free and straight from the shoulder, well away in the front, hocks well flexed, with straight and powerful leverage and well under the body.

Welsh Pony Not exceeding 13·2 hands high. (Section B of the Stud Book)

The description of the ponies in Section A of the Stud Book is applicable to those in Section B, but more particularly the Section B pony shall be described as a riding-pony, with quality, riding action, adequate bone and substance, hardiness and constitution, and with pony character.

Breed Society: The Welsh Pony and Cob Society.

Thousands upon thousands of years ago—no one knows exactly when—prehistoric artists drew pictures on the walls of caves, pictures of animals they saw in their daily lives, and most likely hunted. Some of these ancient studies were preserved, and came to light in the 19th century in Spain and France, and thus are able to tell us across the ages what some of the creatures of those days were like. Among the animals most faithfully reproduced there was a small, pony-like creature with a large, heavy head, rather roman-nosed, and a tufted tail. Apparently the same type roams today the highlands of Central Asia.

In 1881 the skin and skull of one of these animals was obtained by the Russian explorer Colonel N. M. Przevalski, in whose honour it was named

Equus przevalskii. It was described by R. Ly-dekker in *The Horse and its Relatives* (1912) as:

. . . being intermediate in characters between the horse on the one hand and the kiang and onager on the other, having chestnuts on all four limbs. The general colour was described as dun, with a yellowish tinge on the back, becoming lighter toward the flanks and almost white on the belly, with no dark dorsal stripe. The short and up-right mane, which was not continued forward as a fore-lock, was dark brown, and the long coat was wavy on the head. The skull and hoofs were stated to be horse-like.

In 1902 Carl Hagenbeck of Hamburg, of menagerie fame, sent out an expedition to the Gobi to collect living specimens of this wild horse. Adults were unobtainable, but with the aid of a small army of Kirghiz Hagenbeck's agents were able to capture 32 foals. From among these, two colts eventually found their way to the London Zoological Gardens, and two were there in 1977.

Since then this creature has been closely observed and studied, and naturalists generally agree that it is a distinct species and that it has affinity with the various types of prehistoric European horses whose remains have been found at Solutré and other places and whose portraits were made on the walls of the caves of Santander, La Madeleine and elsewhere.

It is about 12 hands in height, has a mas-sive head with small ears and eyes, heavy jaws and unusually big teeth. It has a stocky, rather un-gainly body, with heavy neck and straight shoulders. The tail is tufted, but not in the same way as the ass's; the hairs at its root are much larger than those of the body and rather harsh, merging gradually into the terminal tuft. Legs are fairly slender, pasterns well sloped, hoofs definitely equine. In colour it is dun, with a mealy muzzle, a stripe, black or brown and often very faint, on the back, and some black below the knees and hocks. In summer the mane forms an erect crest, but in the winter, when the coat is long and thick, the mane to some extent falls over on the neck.

Originally discovered in the Kobdo district of Mongolia, north of the Altai Mountains, it moves about in small herds in Western Mongolia, and is very wild indeed and practically unapproachable by man. It interbreeds with the local Mongolian mares which roam those regions in a practically feral state.

Little need be added to this, but attention must be drawn to the influence which the Wild Horse has had, not only with the local Mongolian ponies, as is shown: its type and characteristics are traceable in varying degrees among the ponies of China and Burma and the breeds and types found in the northern parts of India. In addition, and as has been shown elsewhere, many of the North European breeds either trace their descent or have been influenced by Przevalski's horse. Specimens of the true Wild Horse are to be found in different parts of the world, including England, for in Whipsnade Zoo there are several now running in paddocks, having been bred from a stallion, born in Regent's Park in 1931, and a female, given by the 12th Duke of Bedford in 1942. The world count of Wild Horses in captivity in 1977 was 280.

This most useful horse is very little seen nowadays, but originated in that part of Yorkshire which was known as the East Riding (now part of Humberside). For a great number of years it was looked upon as and was indistinguishable from the Cleveland Bay, but it may be safely said that for at least 180 years it had a separate identity.

Going back, then, perhaps to 1790 and for a number of years following that date, the Yorkshire Coach Horse emerged, and the reasons for its foundation were the enormous demands for a bigger, lighter and a more flashy type of horse for the more elegant vehicles which were appearing in fashionable London. For this purpose the basis was the Thoroughbred used with the Cleveland Bay. Records show that the original Thoroughbred sires used for the purpose were 'Necromancer' (1816) and 'Servetur', by 'High Flyer' out of a 'Matchem' mare. Certainly the names of these horses appeared in the pedigrees of well-known early Yorkshire Coach Horses of the period, 'Ebor', 'Paulinus' and 'Seberus', while other Thoroughbred sires associated in the early days of the breed were 'Goliath' and 'Harpham Turk'. However, the breeders of those days were not content only with this cross, but used Arabs and Barbs on Yorkshire cart mares.

The horse was big and powerful, up to 16·2 hands in height, with a long body on comparatively short legs, broad feet, the girth deep, the chest broad and strong, and the shoulders heavy and muscular.

Breed Society: The Yorkshire Coach Horse Society.

The term 'Zebra', a word of Amharic origin meaning 'striped' is not the title of a breed of the horse family but the descriptive name given to the three distinct species of *Equus*, all three entirely unrelated, which have retained the stripes said to have been a past characteristic of other members of the family. Vestiges of these stripes remain in duns, certain primitive pony breeds and in some of the wild ass species, e.g., the onager and the kiang.

From time immemorial, unlike their cousin the horse (*Equus caballus*), the Zebras have inhabited Africa and nowhere else, being found up and down the continent from Ethiopia to the Cape, exclusive of the North African coast. There are a number of local varieties named after their discoverers,

Burchell, Hartman, Grant, and so on, but they are all members of one or other of three separate species: Grevy's Zebra, the Mountain Zebra and the Quagga.

Grevy's Zebra, which is the one illustrated here, is the largest, averaging about 13 hands. Its chief distinguishing marks are long, expanded and round-tipped ears, and the pattern of its stripes, which are very regular and uniform in size, with an almost right-angle change from vertical to horizontal at the head and quarters. The stripes on the neck are broader than those on the body. The longitudinal spinal stripe broadens out considerably on the croup. Its bray is also a distinctive characteristic. It lives on the open, scrub-covered plains in the lowlands of Ethiopia, Somaliland and Northern Kenya.

The Mountain Zebra has its habitat in the mountains of the Cape provinces, Botswana and South-west Africa (Namibia). It differs from Grevy's Zebra in having more pointed and ass-like ears, a slightly more breedy looking head and the presence of a dew-lap on the throat. The stripes are much the same, except that those on the quarters are very broad, and curve more gradually from vertical on the flanks to horizontal on the quarters and thighs. This animal is the smallest of the three species, averaging about 10 hands. It appears to be quite silent, as far as anyone can tell. The late R. I. Pocock, F.R.S., who made a close study of it in captivity states that he never heard it utter a sound.

The Quagga in the past was found in East and North-east Africa, excluding Egypt, very like the Mountain Zebra in appearance, with even more sweeping lines of broad stripes curving from flanks to quarters. It formerly inhabited South Africa as well and was first discovered there, but for some unexplained reason south of the Zambesi it lost most of its stripes, having none on the legs and hind-quarters below the tail and only faint ones on the flanks; but this typical strain is now extinct. It received its name from its very distinctive voice, rather like the repetition of the three syllables, 'qua-ha-ha', which led the Hottentots to call it the 'Khoua khoua', from which the Boers evolved 'Quagga'.

In general all the zebra species are very asinine in appearance, with stocky bodies, heavy heads, very thick necks, straight shoulders and box-like hoofs. Although Hayes and a few others have succeeded at various times in putting odd specimens to drive between shafts, they rarely proved amenable to domestication and training. At one time Zebras, especially the mountain species, were in grave danger of extermination, but it is good to know that these interesting and picturesque members of the horse family are now strictly protected.

It is unnecessary to say that the Zebra is a most remarkable-looking animal, but its fantastic markings are a marvellous camouflage in its natural surroundings. Fortunately Zebras are usually to be found in Zoos, where their strangeness can be contemplated to the full.

With such a vivid appearance, it is obvious the Zebra would be a good act in a circus. Unfortunately, however, the animal is uncooperative and takes most unkindly to any form of tuition. Nevertheless, and it is a great tribute to their trainers' patience and skill, these strange creatures are to be seen in circus acts.

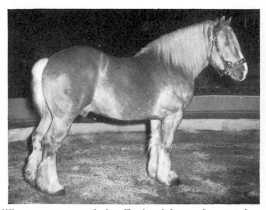

The prototype of the Zeeland horse,* a product of the Netherlands, goes back to the earliest times, and similar types are found in Brabant and Limburg. In the days of the invasion by Julius Caesar, the Romans in 'The Low Lands on the Sea' came across a horse that was very strong and massive; speaking of these fertile lands, so rich in pasture, the monk Saint Winnoq (d. c.715) said: 'There is an island, called Walcheren, which is very rich in foodstuffs and population, where a breed of horses is found, big-sized and of remarkable spirit and strength'. Thus the Zeeland horse became well known at a very early date, and in the Middle Ages it was used by adventurous knights in the wars they were waging,

* The name has disappeared as an official denomination according to the Netherlands Ministry of Agriculture.

and was exported to England, Germany and the western parts of France.

From that time onwards these horses have been in great demand: in the Low Lands as draught-horses; as horses of much use to the farmer in cultivating the land; as animals that could be equally useful in the army for horse artillery.

Since the beginning of this century this horse has been registered in a stud-book (Stud-Book for the Dutch draught-horse, The Hague), so that each one has a number of its own. Breeders give the following details of this type:

Short-nosed head with straight-lined profile; slightly projecting orbit; flat forehead; large, intelligent eyes; short ears, pointing forward; wide, open nostrils; broad, deep chest; close to the ground; very muscular loins, flanks wide apart; very muscular rumps and legs; strong neck of moderate length; plenty of bone with excellent feet and good carriage.

This combination, although sounding unwieldy, is in reality one of some elegance, and on the whole this horse differs from the Belgian by greater elegance and a more lively carriage, while, at the same time, it is bigger than the horse from the Ardennes. In this way people in the Netherlands try to breed a horse, which, though big and heavy, is supple in its movements. It is claimed that the Zeeland Horse can bear cold and heat, possessing great adaptibility under all circumstances. In character it is very suitable for work in the field, being quiet and possessed of much stamina and strength. It is a horse full of spirit, yet very easy to handle.

The wide grasslands of Lithuania have always been
par excellence a fine horse-producing country.
The native breed is known as the Zemaitukas and
has rarely been seen in Western Europe.   The name
comes from 'Zemaitifa', the name for the western
part of Lithuania.   The plural form of the word
is Zemaitukai.

The Zemaitukai are of very ancient origin, and
the two main ancestral strains, those which at all
events have had the most influence on the primitive
type, were the Tartar pony of the steppes
(Przevalski or Mongolian horse) and the Arab,
from animals brought by invading Teutonic
Knights from Western Europe.   The latter was,
and still is, the predominating strain, refreshed by
new Arab stock in recent years.

The appearance of the Zemaitukas is extremely
characteristic.   The prevailing colour is dun, with

light tail and mane; mouse colour is also found and, more rarely, bay. All have a dark dorsal stripe extending to the tail. The head is small, with bright, intelligent eyes unusually widely spaced. The arched neck is short and very muscular, with a thick, wavy mane. The powerful forehand is a distinguishing mark of the breed. The legs are strong and clean, though light in bone, and the hooves hard and well-shaped. The height varies from 13 to 15 hands and the weight from 363 to 454 kg (800 to 1000 lb). In general they are compact, sturdy, well-made animals, full of latent fire and energy, and altogether worthy representatives of the ancient primitive pony type.

It is easy to see to what type the Zemaitukas belongs from this description, which must have become very familiar to the reader, for, with slight variations, it is so similar to what has been written of so many of the Northern European breeds: the dun colour, the dorsal or eel stripe, the short and muscular neck and the thick wavy mane. Like all Russian horses and ponies, many of which are brought up not only in a more or less wild state but subjected to great variations of temperature, the Zemaitukas is one of the toughest horses to be found and owes much of this hardiness to the law of the survival of the fittest which, if it is harsh in itself, has done much in many parts of the world to produce so many breeds of outstanding stamina.

GLOSSARY OF TECHNICAL TERMS

Many of these definitions are based on those given in *Summerhays' Encyclopaedia for Horsemen*

Aids Signals through which the rider directs and conveys instructions to his horse. The hands, through the reins, direct and control the forehand; the lower part of the legs and the heels collect, control and impel the hind-quarters through application behind the girth. The voice is an additional aid; whips and spurs are artificial ones.

Air The correct bearing of a horse in its different movements and paces, being also the correct rhythm to each of these. **Artificial Airs** consist of paces other than the normal walk, trot and canter, and can be obtained from the horse only at the will of the rider and after careful schooling. (See **High School Horse**.)

Ambler see Pacer.

Balance When a horse carries its own weight and that of its rider in such a way that it can use and control itself to the best advantage at all paces and in all circumstances, then it has true balance.

Bang-tail A tail with the hair squared off close to the dock or solid part of the tail. With heavy horses, 'banging-up' the tail refers to tying it up.

Barrel General description of that part of a horse's body which, roughly, is encompassed by the ribs.

Blue feet Dark or off-black coloured feet showing a tendency to blueness.

Buck eye A term applied to a prominent eye, usually believed to be associated with short sight.

Calf-knee Fore-legs which, when viewed from the side and having an imaginary line drawn through them, tend to concavity below the knees. (Also known as **Back-at-the knee** and **Buck knee**.)

Cat-hammed Descriptive of a horse with weak hocks that stand back and away from the natural stance.

Coffin head A coarse, ugly head in which the jowl lacks prominence.

Cold-blood The heavy draught-horse breeds.

Colt A male horse under the age of four.

Concave (dished face) Where the line of the face tends to be slightly hollowed, e.g., the head of the Arab horse.

Conformation General expression to denote the make-up of a horse, whether good or bad, as whole.

Cowhocks Hocks which are turned inwards at the points, as in a cow.

Deep through the girth Descriptive of a horse that is well-ribbed-up with generous depth of girth behind the elbows (see **Heart room**).

Dishing An unlevel and faulty movement of the fore-feet which, when in motion and raised from the ground, are thrown backwards and in an outer circular movement to the front again.

Dorsal stripe A stripe running down the neck and along the top of the body and sometimes to the tip of the tail; generally black, brown or chestnut in colour, and found most often in dun horses. (Typical of horses and ponies of Scandinavian origin.) Also called a **List**.

Elk lip A wide and somewhat loose and overhanging upper lip.

Ewe neck Where the line of the neck from ears to wither is concave. Such horses are said to have their necks 'on the wrong way'. Recognized as bad conformation.

Face Markings These include: *Blaze*, a white marking almost covering the forehead between the eyes and extending down the front of the face across the whole width of the nasal bones; *Muzzle Markings*, including both lips and extending to the nostrils; *Star Markings*, appearing on the forehead; *Strip Markings*, extending down the face and no wider than the flat anterior surface of the nasal bones.

Feather   Hair on all four heels, of varying density and coarseness.

Fiddle-head   A large, plain, coarse and ugly-shaped head.

Filly   A female horse under the age of four.

Flat-sided   A horse is said to be flat-sided when its ribs are not rounded or 'well-sprung'.   Also known as **slat-** or **slab-sided**.

Foal   A colt or filly up to the age of 12 months, described accordingly as colt-foal or filly-foal.

Forehand   The head, neck, shoulders, withers and fore-legs of a horse.

Frog   V-shaped horny substance in the sole of all four feet, which acts as a shock absorber.

Glass, chalk, china or wall-eye   A light blue eye, having a preponderance of white.

Goose rump   Where from the highest point behind the saddle the line runs somewhat sharply downwards to the tail.   Recognized as bad conformation.

Heart Room   A term of commendation indicating depth through a horse's girth, combined with a broad and open chest (**'deep through the girth'**—*q.v.*—is also used).

Height   The height of a horse is taken from the highest part of the withers in a perpendicular line to the ground. The horse is said to stand so many hands (a hand is 10·16 cm or 4 inches), or so many hands and so many inches high.

High School Horse   One trained in accordance with

the principles of the classical Art of Riding and able to perform classical or High School airs.

Hollow Back Where the natural concave line of the back is exaggerated and unnatural.

Hot-blood Horses of the desert and those that are descended from them.

Jumper's Bump A name for the protuberance at the top of the croup, a formation erroneously supposed to increase a horse's power to jump.

Limb Markings These include: *Coronet Markings*, white hair immediately above the hoof; *Fetlock Markings*, around and below the fetlock joint; *Heel Markings*, from the back of the pastern to the ergot; *Pastern Markings*, immediately below the fetlock joint, extending downwards; *Sock Markings*, reaching about halfway up the cannon bone; *Stocking Markings*, extending to the knee or the hock.

Mare The female equine animal.

Mealy nose or muzzle Of an oatmeal colour, running well up the muzzle and having no white markings, e.g., the Exmoor.

Odd-coloured Descriptive of a coat in which there is an admixture of more than two colours tending to merge into each other at the edges of the patches, with irregular body markings.

Over at the knee A forward bend or curve of the knees which may be the result of excessive wear, but is often a matter of conformation. It is a disfigurement which would count against a show horse.

Over bent A term descriptive of an exaggerated collected action with head and neck over-bent at the poll, the chin being tucked into the breast.

Over-collected A horse is said to be over-collected when it shows too much collection, with the head position behind the vertical.

Pacer A horse which, instead of trotting with a diagonal action, moves like a camel, near-fore and hind together, followed by off-fore and hind; this gives a very comfortable gait for long-distance riding and is very popular in America for shows and trotting races. The action is also known as **Ambling**, the old English name for a pacer being an **Ambler**.

Parrot Mouth A malformation of the upper jaw; the incisor teeth overhang the lower jaw and prevent proper contact between the upper and lower incisor teeth. The condition prevents a horse from grazing and may lead to digestive troubles. It is a congenital deformity, and is often called an Overshot Mouth.

Pendulous lip Where the under lip hangs low and lifeless.

Piebald A horse having black and white patches over the body, and perhaps mane and tail.

Pin-toes Toes which turn inwards; horses having such never strike themselves and pin-toes are, therefore, much less serious than those that turn out (**dishing**).

Pulled Tail One where some of the hair at the side of the dock, as well as any excessive growth on top, has been removed by pulling to give a slim and tidy effect.

Quarter Marks Fancy patterns made by brushing the hair in parts with a wet brush in the 'wrong' direction— sometimes a stencil plate is used to help form the design. Seen mostly on racehorses and show horses.

Ragged Hips Where the points of the hips are very prominent.

Roach-back A prominent malformed convex spinal column, also known as **hog-back**.

Roan Colour Where there is an admixture of white hair with the body colour, lightening the general effect of the latter. Thus *blue roan* has black or brown as the body colour, *bay* or *red roan* has bay or bay-brown, and *strawberry* or *chestnut roan* has chestnut.

Roman nose A head with a convex front, found in the cold-blooded horse races as distinct from the hot-blooded races, which tend to the concave; e.g., 'Roman', the Shire Horse.

Short of a rib Where there is a marked space between the last rib and the point of the hip, and showing a sign of slackness over the loins. A condition found in horses of defective conformation, i.e., too long a back, hind-quarters standing too far back.

Shoulders *Sloping*—running obliquely from the point of the shoulder to the withers. In theory, the more sloping the shoulder, the better the ride. *Straight*—less oblique, and should be found in harness and draught horses, where the position and set of the neck collar is important. But a show Hackney must have oblique shoulders for the up-and-out action demanded today.

Sickle hocks Hocks which, when looked at from the side have a sickle or crescent-like appearance, and where the line from the point of the hock to the ground slopes forward.

Skewbald A horse with similar markings to the piebald, only with colours other than black, i.e., brown, bay, chestnut and roan.

Stallion A horse capable of reproducing the species, also known as entire—an ungelded horse.

Standing over A term descriptive of a horse that appears to 'give' at the knees. The defect is not detrimental (except in the show-ring), unless it is caused by overwork.

Tied-in below the knee Where the measurement immediately below the knee is less than the measurement taken lower down towards the fetlock joint. A bad fault and the horse is necessarily light of bone. A horse can also be 'tied-in under the hock', giving an impression of a bad, slightly bent, hind leg. Also known as **Short of bone**.

Toad eye Found only in the Exmoor pony. A distinct and wide mealy rim to both eyelids, and practically running round the eye, which is prominent, thus giving the effect of the eye of the toad.

Undershot Mouth One which is deformed by having the lower jaw protruding beyond the upper with results similar to those caused by **Parrot Mouth** (*q.v.*).

Wall-eye The term used exclusively where there is such a lack of pigment, either partial or complete, in the iris as to give a pinkish-white or bluish-white appearance to the eye. It is not indicative of blindness. Known also as China or Blue Eye.

Warm-blood Most of the saddle and harness horse breeds.

Well-let-down hocks A greatly prized item of conformation. The closer to the ground the hocks are (if unblemished), implying short cannon bones, the better.

Well-ribbed-up A term signifying that the front or true ribs are flat, with the back or false ribs well 'sprung' or hooped behind the saddle, thus providing heart and lung room.

Well-topped An expression to denote a horse that is good in conformation above the legs.

251

INDEX

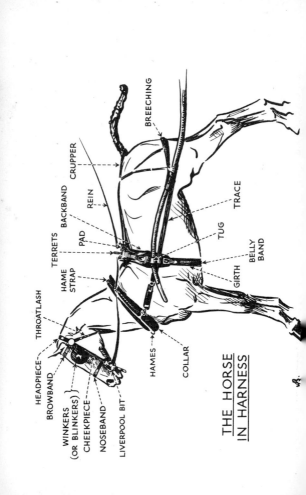

BREECHING

CRUPPER

BACKBAND

REIN

TRACE

TERRETS

PAD

TUG

BELLY BAND

HAME STRAP

GIRTH

THROATLASH

HAMES

COLLAR

HEADPIECE

BROWBAND

WINKERS
(OR BLINKERS)

CHEEKPIECE

NOSEBAND

LIVERPOOL BIT

THE HORSE
IN HARNESS